Sente

for

Admission to Foreign Universities

GMAT, GRE & TOEFL

Prof. A.P. Sharma

Dr. H. Chandalia

Dr. B.N. Soni

UNICORN BOOKS

Distributors

PUSTAK MAHAL®

UNICORN BOOKS, New Delhi

E-mail: unicornbooks@vsnl.com • *Website:* www.unicornbooks.in

©Copyright : Unicorn Books

Distributors

Pustak Mahal®, Delhi

J-3/16 , Daryaganj, New Delhi-110002

☎ 23276539, 23272783, 23272784 • *Fax:* 011-23260518

E-mail: info@pustakmahal.com • *Website:* www.pustakmahal.com

Sales Centre

10-B, Netaji Subhash Marg, Daryaganj, New Delhi-110002

☎ 23268292, 23268293, 23279900 • *Fax:* 011-23280567

Branch Offices

Bangalore: ☎ 22234025

E-mail: pmblr@sancharnet.in • pustak@sancharnet.in

Mumbai: ☎ 22010941

E-mail: rapidex@bom5.vsnl.net.in

Patna: ☎ 3094193 • *Telefax:* 0612-2302719

E-mail: rapidexptn@rediffmail.com

Hyderabad: *Telefax:* 040-24737290

E-mail: pustakmahalhyd@yahoo.co.in

Disclaimer:

ISBN 81-780-6097-3

Edition : 2006

Printed at : Unique Colour Carton, Mayapuri, Delhi-110064

Preface

The questions related to sentence correction are basically meant to test your knowledge of grammar and enhance your communication abilities, which is considered as a strong point for a student of M.B.A. M.B.A. aspirants who take the Sentence Correction Test are required to distinguish an incorrect sentence from a correct one. They are also supposed to know the changes needed to correct any error in the sentences. They are also required to be brief in sentence correction. Errors in such test can pertain to wrong idiomatic constructions, noun-verb mismatches, illogical sentences and superfluous words.

Language skills cannot be mastered overnight. Moreover, you cannot learn everything in grammar in a year's time. You should therefore aim to solve all varieties of questions that appear in GMAT, GRE & TOEFL tests, instead of grappling with the fine points of grammar. The purpose of this booklet is to help you to excel in the questions related to sentence correction test of GMAT. It also helps you to brush up your grammar skills at the same time. Please go through the solved examples and the explanatory answers carefully so as to understand the basics of English grammar.

By the end of the exercise, you should be in a position to identify the types of errors and the correct sentence structure.

Prof. A. P. Sharma
Dr. H. Chandalia
Dr. B. N. Soni

Introduction

Verbal Section

The 'Verbal Section' comprises of multiple choice questions. You are given a fixed time (say 75 minutes) to complete this section. This section judges your ability to understand and evaluate what is written. You are also judged whether you are familiar with the basic conventions of standard written English.

Roughly one-third of the verbal section is made up of the sentence correction section. The questions in this section are developed to test your English usage, your ability to form clear, concise and effective sentences and your ability to choose the suitable word in a given context. You are required to choose an answer that is devoid of redundancies and ambiguities, keeping the basic rules of grammar in view.

This book lays emphasis only on those rules that are likely to be tested in these tests. Such as the GMAT, GRE and TOEFL. You will have to adopt a twin strategy to master this section. If you are able to identify the source of the error, then you will be able to solve more than 80 percent of the questions successfully. So you will have to understand how the English language works. You should not get frustrated by the grammatical terminologies or number of rules that we have mentioned in this book. In fact, understanding of these rules are necessary for solving these questions.

Once you are able to find out the source of the error, you will be able to remove all those alternatives, which are erroneous, thus helping you to narrow down your choices. If you are an avid reader of English journals, then you do not really need the plethora of rules. You can just play it by the way it sounds and mark the one answer that 'sounds' most appropriate. We feel that some knowledge of the rules is needed so that your replies are foolproof.

Given below are some guidelines that can help you to master the verbal section of the GMAT, GRE and TOEFL tests:

1. The error lies in the underlined part of the sentence. These will be no other errors except in the underlined part. However, unless you read the complete sentence, you won't be able to locate the mistake, for the simple reason that the underlined part is connected to the whole.

2. The most common error is no error.

   If you cannot detect an error in the question, you can choose (A) as the answer because the first alternative repeats the underlined section 'as it is'.

3. Do not select the alternative that alters the meaning of the sentences. By the same token, also avoid alternatives that are vague, strange, awkward or repetitive. There may be some sentences that are grammatically correct but change the meaning of the sentence. One should avoid such errors, while solving the verbal section.

4. If you are not able to locate the mistake in the sentence itself, then do not worry. You must then look at the alternatives for clues. Sometimes, by examining the answer choices, you may find a hint to the type of error you are looking forward to in a particular sentence.

5. One should be aware of the common grammar and usage errors tested in these types of competitive examinations. It makes a good sense to have the following checklist of grammatical errors that are commonly tested in these tests:

- **Subject and Verb errors**
- **Tense errors**
- **Pronoun errors**
- **Misplaced modifiers**
- **Comparative constructions**
- **Idiomatic expressions**
- **Commonly confused words**
- **Parallel constructions**

We suggest that you look up a good book on English grammar and go through it properly. This way you can grasp the fine points of the English language. If you are lacking time to do so, then this booklet could give you all the required inputs to tackle the sentence correction section of the GMAT, GRE and such other examinations.

At the end of this book, we have given a full-fledged correction test which allows you to put into practice all the observations you have made in the earlier chapters. You are advised to take the test and refer to the chapters for clarification of errors. **Practice is the only way to become perfect in sentence correction and in the correct usage of the English language.**

Word of Caution: This book is not intended to be a substitute for a proper grammar book. It does not provide an in-depth study of English grammar. **This book simply helps you to succeed in the Sentence Correction Tests of the various competitive examinations such as the GMAT, GRE, TOEFL, etc.** It is not intended to provide you a comprehensive view of English grammar but it acts as a guide to help you in these examinations for **admission to foreign universities.**

∞

Contents

Contents

Parts of Speech

What are Parts of Speech

In English language, certain words acquire different meanings when they are used in different grammatical positions. For example:

Ashok was scolded for his bad <u>play</u>. (noun).

Ashok <u>played</u> the game well. (verb)

In both cases, the meaning of the word, 'play' changes depending upon whether it has been used as a noun (play) or a verb (played). Therefore, the function for which a particular word is used gives it its meaning. The different functions of a word are called the **PARTS OF SPEECH**.

Parts of Speech in English Language

The English language, traditionally has **eight parts of speech**. But in **modern grammar, two more have been added**. Thus, we have **ten parts of speech**, which can be categorized as,

Group A – *Open - class items,* such as:

    i)   ***Noun*** - John, room, question, play

ii) **Adjective -** Happy, new, small, round

iii) **Adverb** - Really, quickly, slowly, then, there

iv) **Verb** - Search, play, grow, look, has, be, do

Group B – *Closed-system items*

i) **Article** - the, a, an

ii) **Demonstrative** - that, this

iii) **Pronoun** - he, they, anybody, one, which

iv) **Preposition** - of, at, in, without, in spite of

v) **Conjunction** - and, when, that, although

vi) **Interjection** - oh, ah, ugh, phew, alas

Group A consists of the parts of speech, which grow in numbers and are indefinitely extendable. It is not possible to draw a list of all the nouns in English. New items are constantly being created and added to the list of already existing nouns, adjectives, adverbs and verbs. **Group B,** on the other hand, consists of those items which can't normally be extended by the creation of additional numbers.

Parts of Speech and Sentence Correction

A sentence is the smallest meaningful unit of a language. *The Parts of speech are the elements of a sentence*. Very often, it is in these small constituent elements of language that major sentential errors occur. A bottom-up approach to the study of the language can help us to tackle and master the sentence correction section. Therefore, it is essential to break up the language into its smallest constituent parts and try to understand each one of them separately.

Nouns

In traditional grammar, nouns are defined as names of persons, places, animals and things, feelings, emotions, thoughts, attitude(s), etc. Non-material nouns are also discussed under the category of abstract nouns. However, the broadest classification of nouns is between **countable** and **non-countable**. There is a great overlapping between the categories of non-countable and abstract nouns. But at times, the non-countable nouns assume countable characters. For example:

Countable Nouns	Non-countable Nouns
Buy an evening paper.	This job requires experience.
He's had many odd experiences.	Wrap the parcel in brown paper.
I've had many difficulties.	He's not had much difficulty.

Nouns may be singular (dog, cat, house) or plural (dogs, cats, houses). A few nouns have the same form when they are used as **singular** and **plural** (deer, sheep, furniture). Some nouns are always used in their **plural** forms (scissors, trousers, pants, spectacles). Nouns which name a group of people or things are called **collective nouns** (bunch, band, mob, troop, herd, etc.), and those which name individuals, persons, unique places, or things are called **proper nouns** (India, John, the Suez Canal, etc.). The names of genre or species are called **common nouns** (book, sugar, water, pen, cow, etc. Feelings, emotions, ideas, thoughts, etc. are given the name of **non-material** or **abstract nouns** (anger, happiness, love, hatred, etc.) We shall discuss the different kinds of nouns, a little later. Let us first indicate what are countable and non-countable nouns.

Countable Nouns		Non-countable Nouns
Singular	*Plural*	*Water*
Apple	Tables	Air
Table	Pens	Sand
Cow	Answers	Grief
Road	Copies	

Proper Nouns	Common Nouns	Collective Nouns	Abstract Nouns
Sita	Pen	Army	Anger
Jaipur	Paper	People	Hatred
Qutub Minar	Cow	Class	Joy

Parts of speech that also function as nouns

Some words in a given situation may take up the function of a part of speech. **Not only pronouns but also adjectives and verbs function as nouns, at times.**

For example:

1. Bangladesh is a *poor* (adjective) country.
2. The *poor* (noun) should be treated with sympathy.
3. The secretary *conducted* (verb) the meeting.
4. He was rewarded for his good *conduct* (noun).
5. Children *play* (verb) and enjoy.
6. The *play* (noun) enacted last night impressed the audience.

Pronouns

"Pro" means 'instead of' and "nomen" means 'noun'. Hence **a pronoun is a word that stands in place of a noun.** The noun that the pronoun stands in place of is called its **antecedent**. For example:

The doctor called the patient in. Then the doctor examined the patient.

The doctor called the patent in. Then *he* examined *him*.

'He' is the pronoun for 'doctor' while 'him' is the pronoun for its antecedent, 'patient'.

The pronouns belong to the closed-system category of the parts of speech. Like their antecedent nouns, they are singular (I, He, She, It, This) and plural (They, We). 'Your' functions as singular as well as plural depending on the antecedent noun for which it is used. **There are eight categories of pronouns:**

Personal Pronouns – I, you, he, she, it, they.

Possessive Pronouns – My, mine, him, his, her, its, their, theirs, your, yours.

Demonstrative Pronouns – This, that, these, those.

Interrogative Pronouns – Who, whose, which, what, whom, why.

Indefinite Pronouns – Anybody, somebody, nobody, none either, each, one.

Reflexive Pronouns – Yourself, yourselves, himself, herself, itself, themselves.

Reciprocal Pronouns – (Showing two people do the same thing).

For example: Mohan and Radha like each other.

Relative Pronouns - (Introducing relative clause)

For example: who(m), that, which, when, why, where, whose.

Adjectives

The word 'Adjectives' comes from the Latin word meaning 'added to'. **Adjective is a word added to a noun and tells us more about the person or thing named in the noun.** For e.g., a lazy girl, a strong boy, a cruel master, a happy wife, a big ship, etc.

The words, 'lazy', 'strong', 'cruel', 'happy', 'big' etc. say something about the nouns – girl, boy, master, wife, ship, etc.

Adjectives can function as 'pre-modifiers' as well as 'post-modifiers', i.e. *they may be placed before a noun or after a noun.* For example:

– We are a small family.

Here 'small'; is a *pre-modifier* as it is placed before the noun, 'family'.

– The house is small.

Here 'small' is a *post-modifier* as it is placed after the noun, 'house'.

Degrees of Comparison of Adjectives

There are **three degrees of comparison of adjectives**, i.e., **Positive, Comparative and Superlative.**

(a) **Positive** – This is the simplest form of the adjective. e.g. He is a *strong* man.

(b) **Comparative** – This is used when two persons or things are being compared. e.g. He is *stronger* than his father.

(c) **Superlative** – This is used when more than two persons or things are being compared. e.g. He is the *strongest* boy of the class.

Examples of the degrees of comparison of Adjectives

Positive	Comparative	Superlative
Good	better	best
Late	later	latest
Old	older/elder	oldest/eldest
Many/Much	more	most
Easy	easier	easiest
Difficult	more difficult	most difficult
Harmful	more harmful	most harmful
Beautiful	less beautiful	least beautiful
Little	less	least
Far	farther	farthest
Thin	thinner	thinnest

Verbs

Words that express an action, a process, a position or state of being are called verbs.

e.g. go, run, read, grind, clarify, be, being, deploy, remember, stay, is, etc.

Verbs have different forms to indicate the time when actions take place. These forms are called Tenses. There are three principal forms of tenses:

Simple Present Tense	:	Asha talks.
Simple Past Tense	:	Asha talked.
Simple Future Tense	:	Asha will talk.

Other varieties of tenses include the following :

Present Continuous Tense	:	Asha is talking.
Past Continuous Tense	:	Asha was talking.
Future Continuous Tense	:	Asha will be talking.
Present Perfect Tense	:	Asha has talked.
Past Perfect Tense	:	Asha had talked.
Future Perfect Tense	:	Asha will have talked.

In addition, there are other varieties like the Present Perfect Continuous, Past Perfect Continuous and Future Perfect Continuous.

The <u>subject of the verb</u> *is the word or group of words that performs the action of that verb.* In the above sentences, 'Asha' is the subject of the verb, 'talk'. Similarly, *the object of the verb is the word or group of words that receive the action of the verb.* In the sentence, 'The horse hit the girl' – The 'girl' is the object of the verb 'hit'.

- **A verb that requires an object to complete its meaning is called a Transitive Verb.**

For example:

The patient needs exercise.

('Exercise' *is the object of the verb* 'needs' and this object is necessary to complete the meaning of 'The patient needs ....').

- **A verb that does not need an object to complete its meaning but makes complete sense by itself is called an Intransitive Verb.**

For example:

The boy cried. (The verb 'cried' *does not need an object to complete its meaning*).

- **Verbs like be is, am, are, was, were, will be, shall be, appear, seem and look are 'Incomplete Verbs'. They need 'complements' to complete their meaning.**

For example:

> The boy **is** smart. (The word 'smart' is needed to complete the meaning of 'The boy is ....')

> In the above sentence 'smart' is a **complement** and 'is' is a **linking verb** (or **incomplete verb**)

(A) **Finite form of the verb**, 'be' – 'am', 'is', 'are', 'was', and 'were' are the finite forms of the verb, 'be'. For example:

– I *am* leaving.

– He *is* crying.

– We *are* going.

In the above sentences, the word 'am', 'is' and 'are' are governed by the **person** and **number** of the subject **(I, He or We)**

(B) **Non-finite forms of the verb**, 'be' – 'being', 'been' are the non-finite forms of the verb, 'be'.

The following sentences show that these forms of 'be' are not governed by the person and number of the subject.

You *will be* coming.

You *have been* beaten.

She *is being* scolded.

We *are being* abused.

Adverbs

An adverb is a word that adds something to the meaning of a verb, an adjective or an adverb. For example:

1. Lizards crawl **fast**.

   ('fast' is the adverb that adds something to the meaning of the verb, 'crawl').

2. He is **very** handsome.

   ('very' is the adverb that adds something to the meaning of the adjective, 'handsome').

3. Handle it **very** delicately.

   ('very' is the adverb that adds something to the meaning of the adverb, 'delicately').

An adverb can modify a phrase or a sentence too. For example:

1. He is **just** in time.

   ('just' modifies the phrase 'in time')

2. **Unfortunately**, she missed the bus.

   ('unfortunately' modifies the sentence, 'she missed the bus').

Prepositions

A preposition is placed before a noun or a pronoun whose relationship with some other word it shows. e.g.

1. The rat is **under** the table.

   'under' shows the relationship between the 'table' and the 'rat'.

2. The boy ran **after** the dog.

   'after' shows the relationship between the 'boy' and 'ran'.

Prepositions can be classified as follows:—

(A) **Simple Prepositions**

   E.g. in, on, with, out, under, till, down, off, since, of, through, etc.

   These prepositions are simple, short words that are elementary, i.e., they are not derived from any other word.

(B) **Compound Prepositions**

   These prepositions are compound words that are made up of words using prefixes. E.g., about, around, into, before, inside, beneath, upto, etc.

(C) **Phrasal Prepositions**

   Phrasal prepositions begin and end with prepositions. E.g. at the top of, by the dint of, by virtue of, in case of, in favour of.

(D) Participle Prepositions

These prepositions are *present participles* in form but are actually prepositions.

E.g. considering, permitting, concerning, owing, during, needing, etc.

Conjunctions

Conjunctions are linking devices. A conjunction is a word that joins words, phrases or sentences.

For example:

Bread *and* butter, Leave it *or* take it,

They may come in between the words/groups to be linked or in the beginning. e.g.

Before she came in, I had finished working on the project.

Although it sounds well, I should show it to the boss before finally approving it.

Interjections

Interjections are *words of exclamations*. They express powerful emotions, be they feelings of joy or pain, wonder or disgust, pity or fear. For example:

Alas! What a pity that he has missed his target again.

Oh! How beautiful!

Note: Each interjection is followed by a sign of exclamation(!)

Exercises

Rewrite the following sentences correctly. Answers are given at the end of the exercises.

(a) Make a list of the content of this box.

(b) What is the criteria of selection?

(c) The staff is having a party this evening.

(d) We lived in Hyderabad since 1987.

(e) I am begging your pardon.

(f) It is harder to be an honest man than to be a successful man.

(g) My loud voice made the asleep students wake up.

(h) Mathematics is more harder than Economics.

(i) That is the man which sold his car.

(j) My brother often is angry with me.

B

Correct the following sentences by putting the appropriate punctuation marks or proper verbs, adjectives, pronouns, prepositions, articles, adverb forms, etc.

(a) I have met him fifteen years ago.

(b) The colleges are closed in the whole of May.

(c) I can concentrate and study well in the night.

(d) Myself, Dr. William-De-Souza.

(e) Will see you soon.

(f) Ram has more confidence.

(g) There are no any books for sale.

(h) He has left for Delhi last week.

(i) Bread and butter are everyone's need.

(j) Oh, what a pity.

Answers

A

(a) Make a list of the contents of this book.

(b) What is the criteria for selection?

(c) The staff are having a party this evening.

(d) We have been living in Hyderabad since 1987.

(e) I beg your pardon.

(f) It is hard to be an honest man than to be a successful man.

(g) My loud voice made the sleeping students wake up.

(h) Mathematics is harder than Economics.

(i) That is the man who sold his car.

(j) My brother is often angry with me.

B

(a) I met him fifteen years ago.

(b) The colleges remain closed in the whole of May.

(c) I can concentrate and study well during the night.

(d) I'm Dr. William-De-Souza.

(e) I'll see you soon.

(f) Ram has much confidence.

(g) There are no books for sale.

(h) He left for Delhi last week.

(i) Bread and butter is everyone's need.

(j) Oh, what a pity!

How to Use Articles Correctly?

The Articles

Articles are **noun markers** as they signal the appearance of a noun. Usually, articles appear immediately before the noun or before some words or phrases that appear between the article and noun.

Kinds of Articles

There are three kinds of articles. The words **A, An,** and **The** are known as **Articles**. **A** and **An** are indefinite articles. They are also known as **countable articles** as they are used before the nouns that can be counted. **The** is a **definite article** which is also known as an **uncountable article**. The word, **'some'** is also an uncountable article. It *is used before the nouns that cannot be counted*. We shall clarify more about the countable and uncountable articles separately with the help of various examples have been given such as:

Simple Examples of Article Usage

(a) A table, a nice table, a beautiful picture, a black cat, an umbrella, an inkpot, an owl, etc. are all examples of **indefinite article usage**.

(b) 'We met a strange man near *the* hospital. *The* man was wearing a red turban.' Both hospital and man with a red turban take the definite article, 'the' before them as they indicate definiteness. The hospital about which the speaker is referring to is already known to the listener. It is therefore, a particular hospital about which a reference is being made. The speaker uses 'the' before 'the man' which implies that he was the same man whom he met near the hospital. Thus, both hospital and man take 'the' before them. We use 'some' to indicate that the number of things, articles or persons under reference is not known or cannot be counted. For example, 'Give me some sugar to make tea for some visitors.'

Conditions for using Indefinite Articles - A and An

A is used before countable nouns giving consonant sounds and **an** is used before countable nouns that give vowel sounds. The following examples will clarify it:

'A man, a book, a chair, a classroom, an umbrella, an inn, an anchor, an idea, an honest person, an honourable man, an orange, etc.'

Therefore, you must remember that **an** is used **before a noun giving a vowel sound. But it is not used merely before a noun beginning with a vowel sound.** For example: 'Words like 'honest' or 'honourable' though they don't start with a vowel, yet they take 'an' before them, as these words start with vowel sounds.

Similarly, to use **an** before a word (noun) beginning with a vowel but not producing a vowel sound, will be incorrect. For example, to say 'an union' or 'an uniform' will be incorrect as both the words don't start with a vowel sound. Let us learn some rules to use articles.

Conditions for using A and An

A and **An** can be used under the following conditions:

- **A** is used with singular countable nouns. Such as 'a man, a woman, a boy, a chair, a library, a classroom, a teacher, a job and a city, etc.

- **An** is also used to display similar situations such as, 'an idea, an umbrella, an elephant, an inkpot, etc.

- **A** or **an** are never used with plural and uncountable nouns. For example, it is wrong to say 'a water, a milk, a liquid, an oil, a paint, a polish, etc.

- There is another rule when you can use **A** or **An.** If the uncountable noun is preceded by a *quantifier* such as 'a gallon of gas, an ounce of salt, a pack of ice-cream, etc., you can use **a** or **an** as required. If you can remember the above rules broadly, you are not likely to make mistakes in the use of the countable articles, 'A' and 'An.'

Conditions for using 'The'

The definite article, **the** can be used before every common noun whether countable or uncountable, but we must keep in mind the following conditions:

- We use the definite article **the** to refer back to a noun that has already been mentioned before. We have already provided a good example above. Let us try to understand it with another example. '*I met a woman in the street, last night. The woman was wearing a black dress. I saw her again this morning wearing the dress and walking swiftly towards the playground.*' When I said 'I met a woman' she was not known to me before. But second time, when I mentioned the same woman and the same dress I had already talked about, I used 'the' before both—woman and dress.

- We use **the** in a context known to the speaker and the listener (writer/speaker, etc.) as mentioned in the above example. Let us examine the same example again. *I met a woman in the street last night. The woman was wearing a black dress. I saw her again this morning wearing the dress and walking swiftly towards the* *playground.*' We used 'the' before the street and the playground, as the listener as well as we knew it well which street and playground they are referring to. Thus, **the** is used in a context known to both the listener and the speaker. It is a kind of identification made to something already known or which is already in the minds of the listener and the speaker.

Conditions where The **is not to be used**

- You should not use the definite article, 'the' without any purpose, as is quite customary with most people for whom English is a second language. For example, 'I met the strange man in the street.' In this case, the correct sentence would be, 'I met a strange man in the street.'

- No articles are used before a proper noun, such as the names of countries, cities and mountains.

- When we mention countable nouns, referring to a class, we don't use the definite article. We also don't use the definite article when we refer to uncountable nouns that possess a 'general meaning.' For example, 'Europeans eat a lot of apples in their breakfast, would be correct, but to say that 'Europeans eat a lot of the apples ...' would be incorrect.

Exceptions to the Rule

- But there are exceptions to these rules. When we refer to the large regions such as 'the U.K. or the USA, or refer to the names of the rivers, such as, the Ganges, the Yamuna, etc., we use the definite article. We also use a definite article before the single entities such as 'the sky, the sun, the earth, etc.

- No articles are used before common nouns except when a special function is denoted. For example, '*She went to bed. It means, she went to sleep.*' But if we say, '*She went to the bed,*' it would mean she reached the bed.' Another example, '*Ramesh is at school.* But if we say, '*We shall meet him at the school,*' would simply refer to the meeting place, i.e. the school.

Exercises

Note: *Please rewrite the following sentences by inserting or dropping articles wherever necessary. Look at the answers only when you have finished the exercises.*

1. There is the dirt on the door.

2. Give him the glass of the milk and put a sugar in it.

3. Give him some ink to write the letter.

4. She gave me books last night.

5. The good student is never late for the lessons.

6. The banana has the sweet taste.

7. She always likes to read the books in restaurant.

8. Please give her the food and the cup of milk.

9. An door of living room is wide open.

10. A youngest son is at the college now.

11. The birds can fly very high in sky.

12. The horses are animals.

13. The girls wear the beautiful dresses.

14. The children love the sweets.

15. She has pen and a piece of paper.

16. The Indian sheep give us a good wool.

17. The bread is made with the floor, sugar and the milk.

18. She wants the doll with blue eyes.

19. A car she drives often makes a loud noise.

20. Please write your name legibly on blackboard.

21. There is the cinema hall behind a red house.

Answers

1. There is dirt on the door.

2. Give him a glass of milk and put some sugar in it.

3. Give him some ink to write a letter.

4. She gave me the books last night.

5. A good student is never late for the lessons.

6. A banana has a sweet taste.

7. She always likes to read (some) books in a restaurant.

8. Please give her food and a cup of milk.

9. The door of living room is wide open.

10. The youngest son is at college now.

11. Birds can fly very high in the sky.

12. Horses are animals.

13. Girls wear beautiful dresses.

14. Children love sweets.

15. She has a pen and a piece of paper.

16. Indian sheep give us good wool.

17. A bread is made with flour, sugar and milk.

18. She wants a doll with blue eyes.

19. The car she drives often makes a loud noise.

20. Please write your name legibly on the blackboard.

21. There is a cinema hall behind the red house.

3 Structure of Varied Sentences

Sentences

When we speak or write, we use a group of words that makes a sentence. For example:

John is going to school.

Sheela has finished her work.

However, if we use the same group of words as under, it does not make a sentence.

To is John school going.

Sheela her work has finished.

Do the above sentences make any sense? Certainly not. Therefore, until we use words in a certain fixed pattern or order, with proper punctuation, it will not make any sense. Let us examine 'what is a sentence?'

A sentence is a group of words which conveys a complete meaning when used in a certain fixed pattern or order based on grammar as well as based on complete sense.

Every sentence must have a subject and a predicate, which essentially contain a finite verb. A subject is a person or a thing we are speaking about. The words that tell something about the subject, is called a predicate. Hence, each sentence has two parts.

For example:

Subject	Predicate
Birds	fly.
My brother	has passed
The old man	had no son.

In this chapter, we shall discuss broadly two categories of sentences — **Sentence Patterns & Sentence Structures**.

Sentence Pattern

A sentence may contain any or all of the following **five elements, such as, subject, verb, object, (direct & indirect), complement and adverbial.**

1. Subject

We may call it the *heart of a sentence*. It is the most essential part of a sentence. It is mainly **a word** or a **group of words** about which the sentence is. Usually, a sentence begins with a subject such as,

Prakash has a good memory.

Borrowed garments never fit well. .

Sometimes, a subject can be put at the end of a sentence too.

Down went *the Royal Convoy*.

Sweet are the uses of *adversity*.

Certain sentences start with a verb and the subject is omitted. For example:

Sit down. (The subject 'you' is left out.)

Thank you. (The subject 'I' is left out.)

2. Verb

It is the second most important element of a sentence. Each sentence must contain atleast a **finite verb**. For example, She *is singing*. ('She' **is a subject**, and 'is singing', **a verb**)

How old *are* you?

Please *lend* me your pen.

How beautiful you *look*!

3. Object

Most transitive verbs take an **object**. *Transitive* means *passing over* and *transitive verbs* are those verbs that denote an action which *passes over* from the doer (subject) to an object. These objects are of two kinds: Direct Object and Indirect Object.

(a) Direct Object

It is a word, a phrase or a clause affected by a verb.

He teaches *English*.

He gave a *book*.

No one knew how to make a *beginning*.

I said that I would never understand *that*.

In order to identify a direct object, better ask a question beginning with 'what' 'who' or 'why', etc. It will immediately help you to know the object. For example:

He gave, what? The answer is – 'book'.

No one knew, what? It is 'how to make a beginning'.

(b) Indirect Object

It is a person or thing for whom or which the action is performed. For example:-

He gave *me* a book.

He teaches *us* English.

In order to identify an indirect object, you may ask a question for whom the action is being performed. For example:

To whom was the book given? Answer is 'me'. Hence, *'me'* is the indirect object. It should be remembered that **an indirect object always precedes a direct object.**

The teacher gave *me* a price.

The mother told *us* a story.

Who teaches *you* mathematics?

4. Complement

A sentence is usually complete with a subject, verb and object, but sometimes, it does not make a complete sense even if these elements are present in a sentence. In that case, we add some words to make a complete sense. The words, which complete the sense, function as a *complement*. For example:

The boys made Rama *captain*.

She made him *laugh*.

The baby seems *happy*.

The cup is full *to the brim*.

The rose smells *sweet*.

5. Adverbial

An adverbial phrase, adverb or adverb clause used in a sentence, is known as an **adverbial**. There may be more than one adverbial in a sentence such as:

She runs *quickly*.

I have done well *on the whole*.

Since you have done this, *I shall punish you*.

Thus, a sentence is made up of *five elements* only. With the addition of each element, a sentence becomes relatively more narrative and it conveys clear & multiple information. Most of the sentence construction errors are natural and connected with the five elements. Let us examine what a sentence structure is.

Sentence Structure

Sentences are of three types—-*Simple, Compound and Complex*.

Simple Sentence

It has only one **finite verb**. In other words, a simple sentence consists of a subject and a predicate.

> *The Moon was bright.*
> (subject) (predicate)

> They played football.
> (subject) (predicate)

Compound Sentences

A compound sentence consists of two or more than two simple sentences. For example:

The moon was bright and *we could see our way.* This sentence has two main clauses. Each has a finite verb. Both of them are linked with *and.* Such sentences may have more than two simple sentences, but each sentence must have a finite verb. For example:

The moon was bright, the sky was clear and *we could see our way.*

The sun set and *the night came on. Men may come* and *men may go* but *I stay on forever.* In the above compound sentence, each clause is independent and makes a complete sense.

Complex Sentences

It has one main clause and one or more than one subordinate clause. For example:

   I returned home as *I was tired.*

   (main clause) (subordinate clause)

Clauses

In the above sentence, there are two finite verbs, which means two clauses. 'I returned home' is the main clause. It makes a complete sense. Therefore, it is independent in itself. '*As I was tired*' is a dependent or subordinate clause because it does not make a complete sense. **A subordinate clause may be a noun clause, adjectival clause or an adverbial clause.** Let us discuss these three types of clauses.

Subordinate Noun Clause

It performs the role of a noun in a complex sentence. It can occur in the following positions as:

(a) The subject of a verb: *What he said* was true.

(b) The object of a verb: No one knows *who he is.*

(c) The object to a preposition: There is no meaning in *what you say.*

(d) The complement to a verb: This is exactly *what everyone can understand.*

(e) In apposition to a noun or pronoun: The report *that he had submitted* is false.

Subordinate Adjectival Clause

Its function is that of an **adjective**, i.e., to tell something about a noun or pronoun. For example:

The *house we lived in* has been sold.

He is the boy *who stood first* in the class.

Subordinate Adverbial Clause

It performs mainly the function of an **adverb** adding to the meaning of the verb. Please see the examples given below.

Don't talk *while she is singing.*

(Adverb of time)

You may put it *where you like.*

(Adverb of place)

Write it down *lest you forget all about it.*

(Adverb of purpose)

He will succeed *as he works hard.*

(Adverb of cause).

I will do this *if I am allowed.*

(Adverb of condition)

He worked so hard *that he was quite tired.*

(Adverb of effect)

He was so weak *that he could not even walk.*

(Adverb of result)

Ram is honest *although he is poor.*

(Adverb of contrast)

He likes you more *than (he likes) me.*

(Adverb of comparison)

Even if it rains I shall come.

(Adverb of concession)

Men will reap *as they sow.*

(Adverb of manner)

Phrases

A phrase is a combination of words that make some sense but not a complete sense. It may also contain non-finite verbs (not affected by a person and number of the subject) such as, 'in the corner', 'on the table', and 'a *smiling* face', 'a good *looking* person', etc.

Like a clause, a phrase may also function as a noun, an adjective or an adverb. Remember that a phrase will either *have a subject or an object*. It will never have both. In case it has both, it will not be treated as a phrase but will be known as a **clause**. Phrases are of three types such as, noun phrase, adjectival phrase and adverbial phrase.

Noun Phrase

Your mother will not do this for you.

Our duty is to **serve *our country***.

He wants *to go home*.

Adjectival Phrase

He is a *good looking* man.

She has a ring *made of gold*.

I like to see a face *with a smile on it*.

Adverbial Phrase

I have done well *on the whole*.

She left *at sunrise*.

He fell *to the ground*.

A phrase may include a non-finite verb at times but never a finite verb.

Non-finite verbs are of three types: The Infinitive, The Gerund and The Past Participle.

I. The infinitive

It is usually preceded by 'to' and functions as a noun/ pronoun in a sentence. **In short, the infinitive is a verb + noun.** For example:

To err is human.

Birds love **to sing**.

They always tried **to find** fault with me.

The speaker is about **to begin**.

II. The Gerund

It is that form of a verb, that *ends in '-ing'* and works as *a verb + noun*.

Sleeping is necessary for health.

Seeing is believing.

I like **reading** poetry.

III. Past Participle

It is the form of verb which usually ends in –ed, -d, -t, -en or –n. It is also known as Verbal adjective. For example:

A **retired** officer lives nearby.

A *failed* candidate, a *faded* rose, a *fallen* city, etc.

While using past participle, we must remember the following:

(a) **If a verb is transitive (having an object), the past participle will never be used in active voice, but only in passive.**

Iron is a metal **dug**_out of the earth.

(b) If the **verb is intransitive, past participle is not used** at all. In case, if it is used as a participle, it must precede a noun and should not be followed by it. For example:

The *departed* guest.

The *dead* horse.

An *abandoned* house.

(c) It is sometimes used to express some permanent habit, state, or character. For example:

A well *read* man.

An out *spoken* lady.

A *broken* heart.

Exercises on the Material Studied

Please identify the right clauses in the following sentences. Answers are provided at the end of the exercises. Please read the example carefully to enable you to answer the questions.

Example

What he said was true. (Noun clause)
(Noun/Adverb clause).

I make friends, *wherever I go.*

(Adverb clause of Place)
(Adverb clause of time/place).

Exercises

1. Don't talk *while she is singing*. (Adverb clause of time/purpose).

2. Write it down *lest you should forget* all about it. (Adverb clause of time/purpose/place).

3. He thinks *because he is rich,* he can buy justice. (Adverb clause of purpose/cause or reason).

4. *Where you live*, I'll live. (Adverb clause of time/place).

5. *As you sow,* so shall you reap. (Adverb clause of purpose/manner).

6. You can pass *provided you work hard.* (Adverb clause of manner/condition).

7. She is younger *than she looks*. (Adverb clause of degree or comparison/ manner/condition).

8. He was so tired *that he could hardly walk.* (Adverb clause of manner/result).

9. *Even if I fail* I shall not give up hope. (Adverb clause of purpose/contrast or supposition).

10. *Why she told a lie* is not clear. (Noun clause/Adverb clause).

11. No one knows *who she is*. (Noun clause/Adjective clause).

12. This is the place *where I was born*. (Noun clause / Adverb clause).

13. He is a man *whom we all respect*. (Adjective clause / Adverb clause).

14. He saves money *that he may grow rich*. (Noun clause / Adjective clause).

15. He is as foolish *as he is lazy*. (Noun clause / Adverb clause).

16. He saves money *that he may grow rich*. (Adjective clause/Adverb clause)

17. I hate such men, *as are falls to their friends*.(Noun clause/Adjective clause)

18. Pay attention *to what your teacher says*. (Noun Clause/Adjective clause)

19. Do *as you like*! (Adverb clause/Noun clause)

20. She began to pray *that God might forgive her*. (Noun Clause/Adverb clause)

Answers

1. Adverb of Time
2. Adverb of Purpose
3. Adverb of Cause/Reason
4. Adverb of Place
5. Adverb of Manner
6. Adverb of Condition
7. Adverb of Degree
8. Adverb of Result
9. Adverb of Contrast/Supposition
10. Noun Clause
11. Noun Clause
12. Adverb Clause
13. Adjective Clause
14. Noun Clause
15. Adverb Clause
16. Adverb Clause
17. Adjective Clause
18. Noun Clause
19. Adverb Clause
20. Noun Clause

Agreement of Verb with Subject

The GMAT is intended to test your knowledge of standard English along with the basic rules that govern the usage of standard English. Thus, if a student seriously learns these rules of correct English, it will prove to be most beneficial to him/her. All one needs to know is how the language works regarding its agreement of the subject with the verb and tenses, use of pronouns and adverbs, use of other parallel constructions, sentences of comparison and idiomatic expressions. The areas mentioned above are the basic areas that are tested in the GMAT.

Having learnt fully well about all the important grammatical rules in the areas mentioned above, it will be easy for you to locate the errors contained in a sentence. It will then help you in constructing a better and a meaningful sentence. This chapter especially deals with the rules that govern the principles of Subject – Verb agreement. *The verb should agree with its subject in number and person as well.*

Rule-1

(a) *A singular subject takes a singular verb and a plural subject is followed by a plural verb form.* **This is called the Subject-Verb Agreement.** For example:

Deepak is reading a storybook.

There is a playground beside the main school building.

Boys are playing football.

There are twenty boys in my class.

The stars shine in the night.

(b) *Two or more singular subjects joined by 'and' take a verb in the plural.* For example:

Kapil and Shyam are friends.

He and I are classmates.

Mohan and his sister have gone to school.

(c) *If two singular nouns, joined by 'and' refer to the same person or thing, the verb is singular.* For example:

The great orator and poet is dead.

The Secretary and Treasurer is absent.

Notice that the verb 'is' used only once when the two nouns refer to the same person. If different persons are referred to, a plural verb will be used for the nouns.

The orator and the statesman are dead.

(d) ***If two singular nouns are joined by 'and', express one idea, the verb is singular.*** For example:

Slow and steady wins the race.

Truth and honesty is the best policy.

Curry and rice is my favourite food.

(e) ***The verb is usually singular, when 'each' or 'every' follows a singular subject. Or, if a singular subject is preceded by 'each' or 'every', the verb is usually singular.*** For example:

Every man, woman and child was happy.

Each day and night is pleasant in the spring.

Every boy and girl was present in the meeting.

Rule-2

When two subjects are joined with, as well as, or together with, the verb should agree with the first subject. For example:

The house, with its furniture was burnt.

The captain, with all his men, was drowned.

Hari, as well as Anil, likes music.

Sita, and not you, has solved this problem.

Rule-3

(a) **Two or more singular subjects connected by or, nor, either... or, neither....nor, not only....but also, take a verb in the singular.** For example :

Ram or Shyam is to blame.

Either Sita or Leela was singing a song.

Either Gopal, Mohan or Sohan has done this.

Neither Raman nor Balu was present.

Not only Ram, but Sohan was also present there.

(b) **If one of the subjects is in the plural, verb must be in *plural and the plural subject must be placed next to the verb*.** For example:

Gopi or his friends have done this.

Either Shyam or his parents were given a prize.

Neither Ali nor his friends are present.

(c) **When two subjects are joined by 'or' or 'nor' and indicate different persons, the verb agrees with the subject nearest to it.** For example:

Either he or I am mistaken.

Neither Daleep nor you are guilty.

But such sentences can be put in a better way as –

Neither Daleep is guilty nor you are.

Rule-4

Either, neither, each, every, every one, and many a, must always be followed by a verb in the singular. For example:

Either of the two boys has done this.

Neither of the two boys has done this.

Each of the boys was clever.

Every boy and every girl was given a prize.

Every one of them has told a lie.

Many a boy has not done his duty.

Rule-5

A Collective Noun (like committee, assembly, congress, jury) may take a singular or a plural verb. If the collection is thought of as a whole, a singular verb is used, but if the individuals or members of the group are thought of separately, a plural verb is used. For example:

The committee have decided this.

The jury has given its verdict.

Note: 'The committee have decided this,' means ' the members of the committee have decided this'. Similarly :

'The jury has given its verdict' means 'the members of the jury are not divided in their verdict.'

Rule-6

(a) Some nouns, which are plural in form but singular in meaning, take a singular verb. For example:

No news is good news.

Mathematics is a difficult subject.

The wages of sin is death.

(b) Some nouns, which are singular in form but plural in meaning, take a plural verb. For example:

According to the present market rate, twelve dozen cost rupees one hundred.

Rule-7

(a) *When the plural noun is the name of one thing (say, a book or a country), it takes a singular verb.* For example:

The Arabian Nights' is a storybook.

The United States has a big army.

(b) *When the subject of a verb is a relative pronoun, the verb must agree with the number and person with the antecedent of the relative Pronoun.*

♦ 54 ♦

(Antecedent means – A thing coming before something else). For example:

I, who am your friend, will help you through thick and thin.

You, who are my friend, should not blame me.

He, who is my friend, should stand by me.

She is one of the bravest women that have ever lived.

Rule-8

The verb must always be made to agree with its proper subject instead of with a noun near it. For example:

The *quality* of these mangoes **is** good.

The *behaviour* of the children **was** praise-worthy.

Rule-9

The case of 'each' and 'none' is slightly complicated. 'None' is not always singular, it could be either singular or plural, depending upon the context in which it is used. For example:

(a) None of the horses **were** injured.

(b) None of the food **was** eatable.

(c) None of the glasses **were** dirty.

The above sentences give the impression of many glasses or the condition of all the glasses:

Whereas in the sentence — none of the glasses was dirty — has the effect of individualizing each glass.

In case of 'each', the word takes a singular verb, when it is subject of a sentence, acting as a pronoun as in – "Each was given ninety seconds to paint a doll".

But when 'each' is used as an addition to a subject, it takes a plural verb as in – We each were given ninety seconds to paint the doll.

Rule-10

(a) *If a subject consists of a collective (noun + of + plural noun) noun such as 'bunch of keys', it will take a singular verb.* For example:

The bunch of keys is lost.

A herd of cattle grazes in his fields.

(b) *If a collective noun is used as a subject and indicates a single unit, it is appropriate to use a singular verb.*

For example:

The team **is** unhappy at the remarks of the coach.

However, when we say, 'The members of the team **were** unhappy with the remarks of the coach,' we will use a plural verb.

(c) There is a subtle difference in the use of the phrases 'a number of' and 'the number of'.

In the sentence, 'A large number of books were ordered by the library', the phrase, 'a number of' is clearly plural. However, the expression 'the number of' is distinctly singular. 'The number of' library members has been declining over the years.

Rule-11

(a) A singular verb is needed after 'one of + plural noun', and a plural verb is needed after 'more than one of + plural noun'. For example:

Ram is one of those students who rarely sings.

Here is one of the pens that were lost.

Concluding Remarks

You will find often that the sentences that appear in the GMAT test will tend to be long where the subject and the verb are separated by redundant or superfluous phrases or subordinate clauses, some of them dealing with plural matters, while the subject is singular. You need to arrive at the 'subject' and the 'verb' that goes with it, apply the rules described in the chapter and find out whether the subject and the verb are in agreement with each other.

Due caution must be exercised. The initial thing in sentence correction is to see whether the subject and the verb are in agreement. If they don't agree, then the first part of detecting the error has already been done. If you find that there is no error in the subject-verb agreement, you need to check the tenses of all the finite verbs.

Apply all the given rules in this chapter with due case and diligence in order to correct the long sentences.

Exercises

Supply an appropriate verb at the missing place in each of the following sentences.

1. No news ....good news.

2. She is one of the best members that ....ever lived.

3. The chief, with all his men,..........massacred.

4. Justice, as well as mercy,.................it.

5. Each of the sisters..............clever.

6. The quality of the mango..........not good.

7. Neither of the men..........very tall.

8. "Gulliver's Travels"..........written by Swift.

9. The wages of sin..............death.

10. According to the present market rate, twelve dozen ....rupees one hundred.

11. The fleet.................set sail.

12. The military......................called out.

13. The crew..................large.

14. The crew ....taken prisoners.

15. He and I ....well.

16. You and he.................birds of the same feather.

17. Either he or I..................mistaken.

18. Neither you nor he............to blame.

19. Ram or his brothers............done this.

20. No nook or corner...............left unexplored.

Answers

1. is, 2. have, 3. was, 4. allows, 5. is, 6. was, 7. was, 8. is, 9. is, 10. cost, 11. has, 12. were, 13. was, 14. were, 15. are, 16. are, 17. am, 18. is, 19. have, 20. was

OO

Tenses and Parallel Constructions

A tense is usually described as a form of verb, which indicates the time of an action. But this is only half the truth. *A tense in its real sense is a grammatical category, which expresses much more than the time of an action.* It tells about the aspects (progressive, perfect, the mood, conditions, completion, non-completion of an action, process, etc. Though there are several rules regarding the uses of tenses, it is pertinent to discuss a single rule, which can help one to avoid errors in the use of tenses.

Rule

If a sentence starts with a particular tense, the same tense should be carried forward in the rest of the sentence. In other words, all the finite verbs in a single sentence must have the same tense. For example:

When she **is** given any responsibility, she **carries** it out to the best of her abilities and always **did** her work in time too.

In this sentence, the first two clauses have present indefinite tense while the tense in the last clause is in past tense, which is incorrect. In order to correct it, the same tense should be used throughout.

For example:

*When she **is** given any responsibility, she **carries** it out to the best of her abilities and always **does** her work in time too.* Another example:

Subhash will be relaxing in a pleasant climate in Simla while we perspire in the scorching heat of Delhi.

The rule says that the future continuous tense used in the first part of the sentence should continue till the end.

Subhash will be relaxing in a pleasant climate in Simla while we will be perspiring in the scorching heat of Delhi.

Exceptions to the Rule

1. The use of past perfect

When two events take place in past, one followed by the other, the previous event will take a verb in past perfect while the later will take a verb in the simple past. For example:

The train had left the station when we reached the platform.

The patient had already died before the doctor arrived.

2. The difference in time

When there is a definite difference in time, between now and then or when action is clearly shown to precede the other in terms of a definite time frame, a present tense verb can sometimes be used to refer to events occurring in past or future. For example:

*Last year, he could not pass, but this year, he is doing **well**.*

John tells me that there was an accident last night.

Rules about Parallel Sentences

Several devices are used to join sentences. In compound sentences, the coordinate clauses are linked by conjunctions while in complex sentences, the subordinators function as linking devices to connect the subordinate clauses to the main clause.

Parallel construction sentences are those compound or complex sentences that contain clauses /phrases expressing a series of actions set off from one another by commas or conjunctions.

Too busy to pack her things herself,   (Incorrect)
Jessica made a list of things to be taken,
ordered a packed lunch, went into the
street calling a taxi.

In this sentence, four actions are mentioned:

Made a list of things ordered packed   (Incorrect)
lunch went into the street calling a taxi

The first three actions are in simple past but the fourth action is in present continuous tense. According to the rules of parallel construction sentence, all phrases of a sentence must have similar phrase structures. Therefore, the verb in the last part of the sentence should be in the past tense.

Too busy to pack her things herself,   (Correct)
Jessica made a list of things to be taken,
ordered a packed lunch, went into the
street and called a taxi.

The same rule can be illustrated by using a few more examples.

The shorter the speech is, people understand it easily.

This sentence is incorrect, as the phrase in the second part of the sentence doesn't match the structure of the first part. It should be:

The shorter the speech, the easier it is (for the people) to understand it.

Rule-1

In parallel sentences with single words or phrases, one should not mix the forms. For example:

Rahul likes to swim, playing cricket and go out with friends in the evening.

This sentence is an example of the mixed forms, hence it does not contain parallel construction. In order to correct it, one should write it as follows:

Rahul likes to swim, to play cricket and to go out with friends in the evening.

Parallel Construction with Clauses

As with phrases, the rules of parallel construction apply to clauses as well. For example:

Pramila was happy caring for her family, looking after her parents and to watch television.

To make it a correct sentence with parallel construction, it should be written as:

Pramila was happy when she was caring for her family, when she was looking after her parents and watching television.

If the voice of the two clauses in a sentence is different, then also the sentence is incorrect. For example:

The collector liked the proposal and
it was supported by the MLA too.   (Incorrect)

It should be written as

The collector liked the proposal and
the MLA supported it too.   (Correct)

A Note for the Examinees

Both the errors pertaining to tenses and parallel constructions are easy to locate. When you go through a sentence for the first time and see a series of actions or two/three clauses constructed in a similar fashion, then you know that it is a parallel construction. Therefore, what you have to do is to find out where the form differs and mark the one which has a similar construction to that of the other phrases/clauses. If the sentence does not appear to be in the form of a parallel construction, then find out whether all the finite verbs possess the same tense. In case, they do not, then see if there is a clear-cut variation in terms of the time gap. If such a variation does not exist and the verbs don't match, then check up the options to determine whether there is an option which has a similar tense. This is in fact the right answer.

Exercises

Correct the following sentences. Answers are given at the end of the exercises.

1. When John is given any assignment he does it timely and completed it in all respect.

2. Ram gave the staff a luxurious party giving them expensive gifts too.

3. When the boss reached office all the clerks are playing cards.

4. The principal started praising his school, showing the photographs appreciated its garden too.

5. The members of the committee found him not guilty, he was acquitted by the Jury too.

6. Children are happy to watch T.V, play cricket and visiting their friends.

7. Major Singh caught the enemy soldiers, tied them with ropes and bringing them to the quarter guard.

8. The writer writes story, types it and posted it.

9. The University offers courses on literature providing for improvement in language proficiency too.

10. When the inspector arrived the constables are smoking and gossiping.

11. The servant started clearing the floor watering plants and scrubbed the utensils.

12. The painter draws the sketch, mixes the colours and applied them too.

13. The head of the department submitted a proposal, it was supported by the dean too.

14. My friend did not see me for many years when I met him last week.

15. He was extremely annoyed when I reported the matter to him and has fired me.

1. When John is given any assignment, he does it in time and completes it in all respects.

2. Ram gave the staff a luxurious party and gave them expensive gifts too.

3. When the boss reached office all the clerks were playing cards.

4. The principal started praising his school, showing the photographs and appreciating its garden too.

5. The members of the committee did not find him guilty and the jury acquitted him too.

6. Children are happy to watch T.V., to play cricket and to visit their friends.

7. Major Singh caught the enemy soldiers, tied them with ropes and brought them to the quarterguard.

8. The writer wrote a story, typed it and posted it.

9. The university offers courses on literature and provides for improvement in language proficiency too.

10. When the inspector arrived, the constables were smoking and gossiping.

11. The servant started clearing the floor, watering the plants and scrubbing the utensils.

12. The painter draws the sketch, mixes the colours and applies them too.

13. The head of the department submitted a proposal; the dean too supported it.

14. My friend had not seen me for many years when I met him last week.

15. He was extremely annoyed and fired me when I reported the matter to him.

OO

Errors in the use of Pronouns

A proper use of pronouns in English is of great value. *A pronoun is a word that comes in place of a noun.* There are various kinds of pronouns such as **personal pronouns** (*I, me, you, yours, he, him, she, her*), **possessive pronouns** (*my, mine, ours, hers, their, his, yours*), **demonstrative pronouns** (*this, that, those, these*), **interrogative pronouns** (*who, whose, which, what*) and **reflective pronouns** (*yourself, yourselves, himself, herself, itself, themselves*). **There are another kinds of pronouns known as indefinite pronouns.** *We call them indefinite as they reflect indefiniteness when referring to an object, person or a thing (anybody, anyone, anything, everyone, everybody, somebody, something, someone, no one, nobody, neither, either and nothing) etc.* Pronouns used with nouns and do the work of adjectives, are known as **possessive adjectives**. For example, 'This is *his* book.' 'These are *your* books.' Let us examine and try to understand the rules that govern the use of pronouns in English.

Rule-1

Indefinite pronouns always use a singular verb. *When any one of the above referred to indefinite pronouns acts as a subject of a sentence or a clause, it requires a singular verb.* For example, 'Nobody says that he was present in the meeting.' 'Everyone is ready to leave.' 'Everyone has boarded the bus.'

Rule-2

There are good chances to commit errors when two pronouns are used in a sentence as objects. It becomes more difficult and confusing as well when one of these pronouns is 'I'. For example, 'She requested me and my son to come to the theatre.' Both the above sentences are incorrect. The correct form will be as follows:

(i) She requested my son and me to come to the theatre.

It is also correct to say, 'My son and I were requested (by her) to come to the theatre.'

Rule-3

Sometimes a pronoun has a double reference and it becomes difficult at that time to say whom the pronoun refers to. For example,

(i) Some teachers maintain strict discipline in the class and their students dislike it. In this case, it is not quite clear to whom does the pronoun 'it' refers to? Does it refer to 'strict discipline' or the fact that 'some teachers maintain strict discipline'. This sort of confusion needs to be sorted out by rewriting the sentence correctly. Its correct form could be: "Some teachers keep strict discipline in the class and their students don't like that sort of discipline."

There can be more examples of that kind where confusion may occur because of an ambiguous sentence by the wrong use of a pronoun. For example:

(ii) Sheela and Meera went to school early in the morning but *she* could not deposit her fees. In the above case, it is difficult to know who that 'she' is? Therefore, to make it clear it would be correct to say, "Sheela and Meera went to school but Meera (or Sheela) could not deposit her fees." Similarly, when someone says, "Lalita and Lucy are good friends but she is so arrogant at times, that she soon starts fighting." To clarify such a confusing statement, one has to be prudent and make its meaning clear. It would be correct to state, "Lalita and Lucy are good friends but Lalita (Lucy) is so arrogant at times that she soon starts fighting."

Rule-4

Pronouns should agree in person and number. It can easily be clarified with the help of a good example.

It would be wrong to state "One should do their work regularly." The correct form will be, "One should do one's work regularly." Let us examine one more example in this context. " Susheel is a bachelor who is in quest of a good girl for him. So he often tries to look for a good girl whom he could marry. But whenever he meets them, he is unable to decide which of the girls he should choose." This example has one great error. It is the use of 'them', which does not coincide with the noun, Susheel, which is singular in number. Therefore, in place of 'them' one should use 'a girl.'

A final word

A final word about pronouns:

Once you have analysed the subject-verb agreement and the tenses, you then need to see the pronouns and check for the following:

(a) What does the pronoun refer to? Is the antecedent of the pronoun clear?

(b) Does the pronoun agree in person and number with its antecedent. If you feel that the pronoun does not agree with its antecedent, check the options to see which of them corrects the error. If you are able to locate it, then it means you have solved the problem. If the antecedent is pretty clear, then you have to check the options for a pronoun case. If everything seems allright, then it could be a problem of a dangling or misplaced modifier. So let us study that in the following chapter. For the time being, we shall examine the different types of errors (relating to pronouns) in this chapter.

1. Errors in Pronoun Subject-Object

Check if a pronoun is the subject or the object of a verb or preposition. For example:

How could he blame she and he for the accident?

(Incorrect)

How could he blame her and him for the accident?

(Correct)

Another example:

All of us—Ravi, Meera, Alice, and me were on time.

(Incorrect)

All of us—Ravi, Meera, Alice, and I were on time.

(Correct)

2. Errors with 'who', 'whom' as an object

She did not know who I meant.   (Incorrect)

She did not know whom I meant.   (Correct)

They discussed for hours whom was better suited.

(Incorrect)

They discussed for hours who was better suited.

(Correct)

I really did not know who should I blame.

(Incorrect)

I really did not know whom I should blame.

(Correct)

She did not know who she should complain about the electricity failure.

(Incorrect)

She did not know whom she should complain about the electricity failure.

(Correct)

3. Errors relating to Pronoun Subject-Verb Agreement

It is important to understand that a pronoun and its verb agree in number. To eliminate such errors, one should remember that *the following are singular in number*:

anything   anyone   either   each   everyone   everything
neither   no one   nothing   what   whatever   whoever
either...or   neither...nor

The following are in plural in number.

both   few   many   several   others   few

A Few Examples:

Meeta was away from the class but a few was there.

(Incorrect)

◆ 74 ◆

Meeta was away from the class but a few were there.
(Correct)

Either of them are permitted to attend the function.
(Incorrect)

Either of them is permitted to attend the function.
(Correct)

Everyone from this class have to report to the Principal.
(Incorrect)

Everyone from this class has to report to the Principal.
(Correct)

Neither of them are good at debate.   (Incorrect)

Neither of them is good at debate.   (Correct)

No one from the invitees have come to attend the ceremony.
(Incorrect)

No one from the invitees has come to attend the ceremony.
(Correct)

Neither she nor he were able to give a good and proper presentation.
(Incorrect)

Neither she nor he was able to give a good and proper presentation.
(Correct)

However, if the noun immediately preceding the verb is plural, you need to use a plural verb. For example:

Either her mother or her brothers are coming to attend the function.

(Correct)

Neither her parents nor her brother is coming to attend the function.

(Correct)

4. Errors relating to Possessive Pronoun Agreement

Please remember that a possessive pronoun agrees in person and number as well.

For example:

Those of us who are interested in it should inform their director.

(Incorrect)

Those of us who are interested in it should inform our director.

(Correct)

If anyone remains absent, tell the director about them.

(Incorrect)

If anyone remains absent, tell the director about him.

(Correct)

Some of you will be require to clean their own room.

(Incorrect)

Some of you will be required to clean your own room.

(Correct)

Everyone of them should check in his own room.

(Incorrect)

Everyone of them should check in their own room.

(Correct)

5. Errors in the position of Relative Pronouns

Please keep in mind that a relative pronoun refers to the word preceding it. In case the meaning of the sentence is not clear, then take it that the pronoun is placed in a wrong position. For example:

She did not permit to enter the house the naughty children.

(Incorrect)

She did not permit the naughty children to enter the house.

(Correct)

Mixed Exercises on the Errors of Pronouns

Correct the mistakes and rewrite the sentences. Answers are given at the end of the exercises.

1. She is not so poor as me.

2. Satish and me are good friends, but at time Satish gets annoyed with them.

3. No one from the relatives have come to attend the function.

4. Please tell him not to forget to bring mine books.

5. Some of you will require to clean their own room.

6. Reema is as old as her.

7. Please don't leave the house without waiting for Prakash and you.

8. I have two of mine houses in the colony adjoining to your.

9. When did him leave to join the new college?

10. All of us—Mohan, Jatin, Shyam and me—didn't reach home on time.

11. She did not know who I meant.

12. I want to know if you have seen a shirt of me.

13. One must try to do his work regularly.

14. She did not permit to enter the house the naughty children.

15. Neither he nor she were able to give a good presentation.

16. Either her mother or her brothers is coming to attend the function.

17. He was allowed to park the truck inside the building, which was quite convenient.

18. She really did not know who should she blame.

19. Everyone of us checked their rooms in the hotel around 2 p.m.

Answers

1. She is not so poor as I am.

2. Satish and I are good friends, but at times Satish gets annoyed with me.

3. No one from the relatives has come to attend the function.

4. Please tell him not to forget to bring my books.

5. Some of you will require to clean your own room.

6. Reema is as old as she.

7. Please don't leave the house without waiting for Prakash and him.

8. I have two of my houses in the colony adjoining to yours.

9. When did he leave to join the new college?

10. All of us—Mohan, Jatin, Shyam and I didn't reach home on time.

11. She did not know whom I meant.

12. I want to know if you have seen a shirt of mine.

13. One must try to do one's work regularly.

14. She did not permit the naughty children to enter the house.

15. Neither he nor she was able to give a good presentation.

16. Either her mother or her brothers are coming to attend the function.

17. He being permitted to park his truck inside the porch was quite convenient.

18. She really did not know whom she should blame.

19. Everyone of us checked in our rooms in the hotel around 2 p.m.

○○

7 Misplaced Modifiers

Sentence errors take various forms. One of these areas is the placement of modifiers. Such errors result when there is some ambiguity in the meaning of a sentence.

Modifiers

A Modifier is a word, phrase or a clause that adds to the meaning of other words in a sentence. A modifier must have unambiguous relation with other words and be placed as closely as possible to the word it modifies. A modifier placed before the word it modifies is called **pre-modifier** and the modifier placed after it is called a **post modifier**.

There are certain rules, which need to be observed in the placement of the modifiers.

Rule-1

Modifiers must be placed as close as possible to the word they modify. Special care needs to be taken while using the adverbial and adjectival phrases.

For example:

Wanted a tutor for a student, M.A. in English literature.

(Incorrect)

The intended meaning is:

Wanted a tutor, M.A. in English literature, to teach a student.

(Correct)

Another example:

Wanted a maidservant for a baby, 26 years old.

(Incorrect)

The intended meaning is not that a maidservant is required for a 26 years old baby, but it is:

Wanted a 26 year old maidservant to look after a baby.

(Correct)

Rule-2

A Phrase beginning with "As" should never be left unrelated i.e., the corresponding noun/pronoun must be stated after the adjectival phrase.

For example:

As a collector, the tension in the town is a concern.

"As a collector" is a phrase, it must refer to someone. The correct form of the sentence would be:

As a collector, I am concerned about the tension in the town.

Another example:

As a teacher I am concerned about the absence of some students from the college.

Rule-3

If there is more than one noun/pronoun in a sentence then the modifying participle should attach itself to the one which is nearest to it.

The problem occurs when the noun/pronoun to which the modifier is intended to refer is not placed next to the modifier.

For example:

While walking home, the traffic made him halt for more than an hour.

Appropriate changes are required in the above sentence to clarify the meaning.

While he was walking home, the traffic made him halt for more than an hour.

or *While walking home, he was made to halt for more than an hour due to heavy traffic.*

Another example:

While driving the car, the police inspector ordered him to stop.

In this sentence, it appears as if the police inspector were driving the car. The intended meaning, however is:

While he was driving the car, the police inspector ordered him to stop.

While driving the car, he was ordered by the police inspector to stop.

These examples make it very clear that a modifier must have a noun or pronoun to go with it. For correcting the sentences with errors of this kind, appropriate noun/ pronoun need to be placed at the right place.

Let us take another example:

Starting from the railway station, the university can be reached in half an hour.

The modifier 'Starting from the railway station' must be followed by a noun or pronoun to answer the question 'who starts from the railway station?' The error therefore, lies in the second part of the sentence. It would require an addition of a noun/pronoun like visitors/people/one/you, etc.

Starting from the railway station, the visitors/people/you/ one can reach the university in half an hour.

If the modifier in a sentence given for correction is underlined, it has to be revised.

Starting from the railway station, the university can be reached within half an hour.

If the modifier is in the form of a non-finite phrase, the correct sentence should be the one which changes a

non-finite verb into a finite verb with a subject of its own. Changing the phrase into a clause can do this.

If you start from the railway station, the university can be reached within half an hour.

It is just an example of the error of a misplaced modifier. The above mentioned rules are helpful in finding a correct alternative.

Exercises

Correct the following sentences.

1. Wanted a match for a beautiful girl, twenty five years old.

2. Wanted a nurse for a baby, 20 years old.

3. As a teacher, the privatization of education is a concern.

4. As a reviewer, increasing sex and violence in films is a concern.

5. As a political activist, falling moral standards in politics is a concern.

6. While preparing for interview, Mr. Bose gave me certain tips.

7. While visiting the homes of the victims, the public forced him to announce the relief measures.

8. Starting from the market, the secretariat can be reached in twenty minutes.

9. Starting from the college, the university office can be reached in twenty minutes.

10. As a journalist, entry of MNC's in print media is a concern.

11. As a conscientious citizen, rising crime rate disturbs.

12. While reading a book, the students stormed into the library.

13. While taking the examination, Dr. Roy reached his pockets.

14. Wanted a psychiatric doctor for a private clinic.

15. He bought a fresh basket of fruits.

Answers

1. Wanted a match for a beautiful 25 year-old girl.

2. Wanted a 20 year-old nurse, for a baby.

3. As a teacher, I'm concerned about the privatization of education.

4. As a reviewer, I'm concerned about the increasing sex and violence in films.

5. As a political activist, I'm concerned about the falling moral standards in politics.

6. While I was preparing for the interview, Mr. Bose gave me certain tips.

7. While he was visiting the homes of victims, the public forced him to announce the relief measures.

8. Starting from the market, one can reach the secretariat in twenty minutes.

9. If one starts from the college, the university office can be reached in twenty minutes.

10. As a journalist, I am concerned about the entry of MNCs in print media.

11. As a conscientious citizen, I am concerned about the rising crime rates.

12. While I was reading a book, the students stormed into the library.

13. While he was taking the examination, Dr. Roy reached into his pockets.

14. Wanted a doctor, experienced in psychiatry for a private clinic.

15. He bought a basket of fresh fruits.

OO

Comparatives

Sentences or clauses that indicate some kind of comparison are called comparatives. To make comparisons, we often use words like — 'than', 'like', 'as though'. 'similar to'. The usage of comparatives is also ruled by certain basic rules. GMAT tests try to test whether you are aware of the rules that govern comparative constructions.

Rule-1

While comparing two dissimilar things, it is important to bear in mind that we compare certain items having similar qualities or attributes. It can be clarified with the help of a pronoun or a modifying clause. For example:

>It is *as hot as* yesterday.   (Incorrect)

The correct form of the sentence would be:

>It is *as hot as it was* yesterday.   (Correct)

We can give another example of this kind such as:

>The cotton of Japan is superior to Egypt.

It is incorrect, because, it reflects the comparison between 'cotton' and 'Egypt' and not between 'cotton of Japan' and 'cotton of Egypt'. The correct sentence would be:

The *cotton of Japan is superior to the cotton* of Egypt.

Rule-2

Don't compare a thing with the class it belongs to. For example:

Roses smell sweeter than any flowers. It is incorrect because smell and flowers are compared.

Roses smell sweeter than any other flowers do. It is correct because the smell of roses and that of the flowers is being compared. One more example will clarify it further.

Gold is more expensive than any metals.

(Incorrect)

Gold is more expensive than any other metal.

(Correct)

Rule-3

Comparative constructions must not be ambiguous. They should be clear and easy to understand. For example:

He hates television as much as his wife. It is an ambiguous sentence which may mean that 'he hates television and his wife both', or 'he hates television and his wife also hates television'. Therefore, to make the meaning more clear, one must say,

He hates television as much as he hates his wife.

or

He hates television as much as his wife does.

Rule-4

We must be careful to use expressions like 'as good as' and 'if not better than':

For example:

Mangoes are as cheap, if not cheaper than they were last year.

(Incorrect)

The correct form of this sentence would be:

Mangoes are as cheap as they were last year, if not cheaper.

(Correct)

Concluding Remarks

While looking for an error in comparatives, we need to keep in mind that a sentence comparing two things or a sentence having the words such as 'as' 'than', 'like', etc. have been used correctly.

For example:

There were twice as many casualties in the riots this year than in the year before. It simply compares two different things (number of casualties with the year). *So it is incorrect. The correct sentence would be*:

There were twice as many casualties in the riots this year than *those* in the year before.

Exercises

Fill up the blanks with the appropriate adjectives (comparative/superlative).

Example: Which is the ...of the two. (good)

Which is the *better* of the two.

1. He is the ....boy in the class. (lazy)

2. He has seen.......days. (happy)

3. What is the ......news from America? (late)

4. It was the ....moment in my life. (proud)

5. Iron is ....than any other metal. (useful)

6. Mohan is........than any other student. (clever)

7. The population of Mumbai is.......than that of Delhi. (great)

8. Your coffee is not.........than mine. (good)

9. The houses of the rich are...............than those of the poor. (large)

10. Sheela is the ....of the three. (clever)

11. He is the...............of all men in the village. (wise)

12. She is the ....student in the class. (smart)

13. He ran.................than everyone in the class. (fast)

14. She is the ....of all her sisters. (thin)

15. Gold is ....than silver. (cost)

Answers

1. laziest; 2. happier; 3. latest; 4. proudest; 5. more useful; 6. cleverer; 7. greater; 8. better; 9. larger; 10. cleverest; 11. wisest; 12. smartest; 13. faster; 14. thinnest; 15. costlier.

OO

Errors Relating to Idiomatic Usage

GMAT Sentence Correction is extended to test the candidates in the use of idioms and phrases. In fact, an idiom is a phrase or a group of words used to convey some special meaning that cannot be easily understood through a dictionary. *An idiom can be defined as a set of words or a language, which has some specific character and which is peculiar to a country, district or group of people.* Many phrasal verbs such as 'look after' or 'run over', are idiomatic. They convey special meanings and are frequently used when one communicates to the other. Most idioms are formed with the help of prepositions. The use of such idioms is conventional. *There are no rules or assumptions to determine the correctness of an idiomatic expression except that it is used conventionally by some people and carries a special meaning in a particular situation.*

There is a simple way to know the correctness of an idiomatic expression. It is to play by the ear. If you go on using the language correctly and encounter idiomatic expressions in between, it would become easier for you to know which idiom is correct at a particular situation. Only then you can play by the ear. Otherwise, there is no logical way to find out whether a particular idiom is correct or incorrect.

Some of the most common idiomatic expressions that at times may confuse you, are given below. Please go through them very carefully and try to understand them with the help of their usage on different occasions, and consult a good dictionary that gives the meanings of such expressions.

The Phrasal Verbs

Verbs preceded or followed by prepositions are known as phrasal verbs. These phrasal verbs are of two kinds—*inseparable and separable. Inseparable verbs* are generally formed by two words out of which one word is a preposition. *Separable verbs* are formed by a **verb + pronoun + preposition**. The phrasal verbs that are formed by a verb + preposition, are *inseparable.* It will be grammatically wrong to separate them as by doing so, their meaning will be changed. Some common inseparable phrasal verbs (idiomatic expressions) that may be helpful in enriching your language have been given such as:

Phrasal Verbs (Inseparable verbs)	Meanings
Above board	Open, without deception
Agree with	Be of the same opinion
Appeal to	Make an earnest request
Arrange for	To settle or to adjust
Ask for	To invite trouble
Attend to	To give care and thought
Babble out	Talk mistaken or not understood
Back up	To support
Bear against	Having in the heart or mind.
Better of	To overcoming or winning
Blow out	To exhaust itself
Cry out	Crying until emotionally relieved
Call on	Pay a short visit
Care for	Look after
Clear up	Become clear
Direct to	To speak or to put address
Die away	Lose strength
Dig into	To push hard
Drop off	To become fewer or less
Drive hard	To put pressure on someone
Give in	To yield
Go back	Extend backwards in space or time

Hold up	Stop by use of threat or force
Look after	To take care
Pull up	Check, reprimand
Pull down	Weaken (of illness)
Run down	Knock down or collide
Send for	Ask or order to come

The *separable verbs* have also idiomatic meanings and are called phrasal verbs. They are separated (or joined) by a pronoun, a noun, a conjunction or a preposition, but they also form idiomatic expressions. A list of separable verbs (idioms) for the reference of the readers, is given below:

Phrasal Verbs (Separable verbs)	Meanings
Air it out	Expose
Argue it for	Give reasons for
Ask for it	Behaving to get in trouble
Back it up	Support
Bear it away	Carry it on/carry it off
Break it down	Divide, analyze and classify
Be up and about	Be out of bed & become alert
Bring it about	Cause to change direction
Bring it up	To educate, to call attention
Carry it forward	To transfer it to the head of a new page.

Catch it up	Overtaking
Clear it away	Take it away, get rid of.
Close it down	Stop production; shut it down
Cut it out	Remove by cutting
Draw it up	Bring it to stop
Fill it up	Make it, or become quite full
Find it out	To detect a wrongdoing.
Finish it up	Eat up (dinner/lunch/breakfast) completely
Get down to	To start work earnestly
Give it away	Handing over
Get it done	Complete it
Get it off	Save from punishment or penalty
Hand it over	To give it to, to surrender
Leave it out	To omit, fail to consider
Lock it up	Make safe by placing in custody
Look it up	Raise the eyes; search for; pay a call
Make it up	To complete, supply, invented-composed
Make it out	Write out, to complete it, managed to see
Mix it up	To confuse or maladjusted
Pass it out	To faint; leave college having passed
Pay it back	To return

Pick it up	To break up; recover
Pick it out	Make out; choose; distinguish from objects
Point it out	To indicate, to identify, call attention
Put it away	Give up, renounce
Round them off	Bring to a satisfactory conclusion
Round it up	Driving together, bring to a whole number
Set it up	To establish
Take it out	Accept as compensation
Take it in	To receive in place of actual payment
Take it all	Considering everything
Talk it over	Discuss it
Talk it out	Persuade to do/not to do
Think it over	Reflect upon; consider further
Think it out	Consider carefully
Try it on	Put on garments
Try it out	Use it, experiment with it
Turn them away	Refuse to look at it; turning it to different direction
Turn them down	Refuse to consider it.
Turn it off	Stop the flow (of gas)
Turn them over	Fall over; up set, change the position of

Wear them out	Exhaust or tire out
Wind it up	Handle; raise it by doing or handling
Wipe it out	Clean the sides of it
Wipe it away	To remove by wiping
Work it in	Find a place for; introduce into
Work it out	Calculate, devise, to develop, to find a solution

Some Additional Idiomatic Expressions

It has been observed that we often use idiomatic expressions incorrectly. There is no reason for doing so except that it happens on account of lack of reading the right material and not giving attention to the language properly. In order to provide the reader an idea how we often make mistakes in relation to the use of idiomatic expressions, some examples are given below. *These examples will help you understand that a verb when followed by an appropriate preposition or adjective, becomes an idiom.* These prepositions or adjectives have been interwoven into the language with the passage of time. Therefore, they are used conventionally. *Thus, no particular rule or canon can be provided to identify or explain why a particular adjective or a pronoun is used to make an idiom.* Idioms are therefore, the legacy of a country, people or a particular language. The reader is advised to consult a standard dictionary when he/she is in doubt.

1. **Agree with** something means to be willing to accept or to allow something.

   She agrees to my views.   (Incorrect)

   She agrees with my views.   (Correct)

2. **Appeal to** means an earnest appeal/request.

   The mother appealed with the
   principal to pardon her son.   (Incorrect)

   The mother appealed to the
   principal to pardon her son.   (Correct)

3. **Arrange for** means to settle or to adjust; to make plans in advance.

   Sheela has arranged a car to
   receive them at the airport.   (Incorrect)

   Sheela has arranged for a car to
   receive them at the airport.   (Correct)

4. **Babble out** stands for talking in a way that is difficult to comprehend.

   She often babbles so nothing is
   clear to me when she talks.   (Incorrect)

   She often babbles out so nothing is
   clear to me when she speaks.   (Correct)

5. Back up **means to support**

   Seema is my good friend. She always
   backs me on when I need her help. (Incorrect)

   Seema is my good friend. She always
   backs me up when I need her help. (Correct)

6. **Back down** conveys the sense of giving up a claim.

   Although she promised to continue
   as a president of the company,
   she backed out in the last meeting. (Incorrect)

   Although she promised to continue
   as the president of the company,
   she backed down in the last meeting. (Correct)

7. **Bear against** means to have (grudge) in the heart or
   mind.

   Please don't bear any grudge for
   your friends for nothing. (Incorrect)

   Please don't bear any grudge against
   your friends for nothing. (Correct)

8. **Bent on** gives the meaning of having determination

   I am bent to attain very good
   marks in my final examination. (Incorrect)

   I am bent on (upon) attaining very
   good marks in my final examination. (Correct)

9. **Better of** implies the sense of overcoming or winning.

His cowardice got the better in him. (Incorrect)

His cowardice got the better of him. (Correct)

10. **Bound for** means to get ready to start (destination).

This train is bound to Delhi. (Incorrect)

This train is bound for Delhi. (Correct)

11. **Call off** means to call away.

The strike has been called out. (Incorrect)

The strike has been called off. (Correct)

12. **Care about** means to feel interest, anxiety or sorrow.

She does not care much for what
happened to me in the hotel. (Incorrect)

She does not care much about
what happened to me in the hotel. (Correct)

13. **Depend upon (on)** means to rely on or need.

One's good health depends at
one's good habits. (Incorrect)

One's good health depends upon
one's good habits. (Correct)

14. **Deprive of** means to take away from.

She was deprived in books when

she was in high school. (Incorrect)

She was deprived of books when

she was at high school. (Correct)

15. **Ease off** means to give relief to the body or mind from pain, discomfort or anxiety.

Can I ease you from your anxiety
so that you may think properly? (Incorrect)

Can I ease you off your anxiety
so that you may think properly? (Correct)

16. **Escape from** means to get free; get away.

The parrot has escaped away
from its cage. (Incorrect)

The parrot has escaped from its cage. (Correct)

17. **Excuse from** means to get free from a duty or requirement

You are excused to attending
the classes. (Incorrect)

You are excused from
attending the classes. (Correct)

18. **Fall flat** means failing to have the intended effect.

The function was managed so badly
that it fell down at the end. (Incorrect)

The function was managed so badly
that it fell flat at the end. (Correct)

19. Find out means to detect any wrongdoing or error.

She was found while
stealing the papers. (Incorrect)

She was found out while
stealing the papers. (Correct)

20. Finish up means to eat up completely.

The boy was so hungry that
he finished his whole meal. (Incorrect)

The boy was so hungry that
he finished up his whole meal. (Correct)

Common Expressions in English

These expressions are often used either in writing or during conversation. You must keep in mind that these words are framed in such a way that unless you use them correctly they will not provide the desired or appropriate meanings. Some of them are given below with their meanings as well as uses.

As a consequence of
It means **as a result of**. He was expelled from the college as a consequence of his misconduct.

As good as

It means **the same thing as**. She is as good as her brother.

As long as

It means **on condition that**. You will get your pocket money as long as you behave well.

At the most

It indicates **some limit or to an (some) extent**. At the most he can attain the position of a principal but not of a director.

At any cost

It means **by using all sorts of means and ways**. We want to fulfil that mission at any cost.

As soon as

It means **soon**. As soon as she comes home we all will leave.

Better than

It involves a kind of comparison between two things, persons, etc. Hari is better than Mohan in many respects.

In line with

It denotes some sort of similarity or equality. Your decisions are in line with mine.

Not only…but also

It is a phrase that is **used to stress that one more thing or quality or whatever, besides the previous**

one is also there. She not only attended the party, but also sang a song at the request of the host.

Not so much …as
It is also used to show some sort of comparison between two things but in a negative manner. For example, She does not possess so much enthusiasm towards work as you had reported to me. There is not so much water in the lake as you had described.

Responsible for
It relates to someone's liability towards work, or commitment or a person. It can be used in a positive or in a negative sense. For example, She was responsible for ruining his life and future. She worked very hard to help him. Therefore, she was responsible for making his career.

Auxiliary Verbs that make Idioms

When sentences start with verbs like **have, make, take** and **do,** you may make mistakes, as it is tricky to use them correctly. Let us examine them separately to learn more about them.

Phrases starting with 'take'.	Their usage
Take a test	Take a test to know whether you are really good at work.
Take it normally	Take it normally. Please don't mind what he said.
Take it coolly	Take my word coolly. Please don't misunderstand me.
Take to heel	Taking to heels at the sight of the police, the thieves were finally caught.
Take a notice	Take a notice of all what is said to you right now.
Take it well	Take my advice well, for it will help you in future.
Take a shower	Take a shower right now, for it is very hot.
Take it out	Take out these dirty stains from my shirt.
Take down	Take down the entire speech and make a report.
Take into account	Take Deepak into account as he is highly trustworthy.
Take over	Take over from him all the household duties.

Sentences starting with 'do'.	Their usage
Do your duty	Do your duty well.
Do exercise	Do exercise regularly to help you build your body.
Do your best	Do your best to improve your performance.
Do as told	Do what you are told and don't argue.
Do good	Do good to others if you want to live happily.
Do some shopping	Do some shopping in line with our requirements.
Do take it well	Do take well his advice; It will help you a lot.
Do keep silence	Do keep silence as it is always required here.
Do no harm	Do no harm to the poor for they are often unhappy.
Do your job.	Do your job well if you want to progress.

Phrases starting with 'make'.	Their usage
Make believe	Make believe that Shyam is your best friend until I come back to help you.
Make noise	Making noise in the library is not permitted.

Make off	Make off to reach the railway station on time.
Make out	Make out a cheque worth Rupees one thousand.
Make for	Make for the market right now.
Make offer	Make an offer to him to sell the house.
Make up	Make up the sum we need in the theater.
Make over	Make over this place as your study room.

Phrases taking the verb 'have'.	Their usage
Have breakfast	Have some breakfast before you leave home.
Have a bath	Have a bath right now.
Have fun	Have fun with your friends.
Have a lesson	Have a lesson on this topic.
Have a party	Have a tea-party tonight.
Have a programme	Have a nice programme tonight.
Have a class	Have a class tonight.
Have a picnic	Have a picnic with your girl friend.
Have a drink	Have a drink right now.

Test Exercises on this Chapter

Let us take two tests on the material that we have gone through in this chapter. Remember that your good habit of reading will always help you to identify the mistakes hidden in a sentence. Please correct the following sentences keeping in view what you have learnt from the language material given in this chapter as well as in other chapters. Don't read the answers given at the end of the exercises until you have finished them.

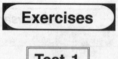

1. The manager of the company appealed with the director to wait for sometime before taking any decision in that matter.

2. It is never advisable to bear any grudge for your friends on flimsy matters.

3. A couple of captives escaped away from the Central Jail last night around twelve.

4. The principal excused Rohit to attending the classes, as he was sick for many days.

5. Sheela was found by her mother when she was stealing money from the chest.

6. As the beggar was extremely hungry, he finished the food in a few minutes.

7. Don't take grudges against your brother for no solid reasons against him.

8. You must make it coolly as such unusual happenings do happen in every family.

9. Take out the details of the project very carefully before you intend to submit it.

10. Go, take a picnic with your friends during the coming Deepawali break.

11. I advise you to take fun at times than to remain doleful everytime.

12. Their plans to visit the Taj during last summer fell down as none of them had any idea what route or how much money was involved in the journey to the Taj city.

13. Meera has arranged a car to receive her uncle from the airport.

14. He is bend to attending the party even if he is not invited.

15. The workers of the factory have called out the strike.

16. She cares much for her mother though she is seriously ill.

17. I shall depend at you to look after my house when I am out of station.

18. When she left home in the night, she was deprived to taking any money with her.

19. He can easily ease me from my problems if he likes.

20. She is not so much good in physics than in mathematics.

Test 2

1. Sitting on the ground a letter was written by her.

2. Ganesh was married with Sheela.

3. He who you helped has turned a union leader.

4. All his hairs are gray.

5. Teacher's room was locked and the teachers had to remain outside.

6. This kind of books are not liked by me.

7. His daughters are beautiful but his sons ugly.

8. The electric bulb was hot to be touched.

9. The M.L.A. had interviewed of the Governor.

10. She is true to her words.

11. The fort is built of bricks, not of stones.

12. He ran a ten-mile race.

13. One of the passengers' daughter got hurt.

14. He wants two breads.

15. It was him who broke the chair.

16. Five hundred miles is a long distance.

17. All but him had run away.

18. She need not to come to office.

19. She is not selfish, nor I am.

20. She spoke very hasty.

21. Call his anything else than a stupid.

22. God may bless you.

23. If you study hard, then you will pass.

24. She tried to quickly cross the road.

25. She is junior than me.

26. Her problem is the same like yours.

27. The clerk copied the letter word by word.

28. What for is Mumbai famous?

29. After 1979, the use of eggs has increased each year.

30. Bangalore is very popular among the people of India.

31. See these phrases in standard dictionary.

32. I am enclosing a cheque of Rs.100.

33. She would like to discuss about what to do next.

34. On every Sunday afternoon she plays tennis.

35. London is far from Delhi.

36. Unless you do not study hard, you will not get good marks.

37. Gopal does not dare come here.

38. "Have you ever gone to Mumbai?"

39. He wants to know as to why he has been detained.

40. She is a student in the university of Jaipur.

41. As it was raining they decided to stay indoor.

42. He arrived in Mumbai on 15th of December.

43. We shall supply you everything you need.

44. He will phone you again in ten minutes.

45. He could hardly believe in his eyes.

46. It is childish to complain against rules.

47. Does your country import something?

48. He sent for the doctor because I am ill.

49. They have each their problems.

50. Will she have to pay custom duty?

Answers

Test 1

1. Appealed to 2. grudge against 3. escaped from 4. excused Rohit from 5. found out 6. finished up 7. have grudges against 8. take it coolly 9. make out 10. have a picnic 11. have fun 12. fell flat 13. arranged for 14. bent upon 15. called off 16. care for 17. depend upon 18. deprived of 19. ease me off 20. physics as.

Test 2

1. Sitting on the ground, she wrote a letter.

2. Ganesh was married to Sheela.

3. He whom you helped has turned a union leader.

4. All his hair is gray.

5. The teacher's room was locked and they had to remain outside.

6. This kind of book is not liked by me.

7. His daughter is beautiful but his sons are ugly.

8. The electric bulb was too hot to be touched.

9. The MLA had an interview with the Governor.

10. She is true to her word.

11. The fort is built of bricks, not of stone.

12. He ran a ten–mile race.

13. The daughter of one of the passengers got hurt.

14. He wants two pieces of bread.

15. It was he who broke the chair.

16. Five hundred miles is a long distance.

17. All but he had to run.

18. She need not come to the office.

19. She is not selfish, nor am I.

20. She spoke very hastily.

21. Call him anything else but a stupid.

22. May God bless you!

23. If you study hard, you will pass.

24. She tried to cross the road quickly.

25. She is junior to me.

26. Her problem is same as yours.

27. The clerk copied the letter word by word.

28. What is Mumbai famous for?

29. Since 1979, the use of eggs has increased each year.

30. Bangalore is very popular with the people of India.

31. Look up these words in a standard dictionary.

32. I am enclosing a cheque for Rs.100/-.

33. She would like to discuss what to do next.

34. Every Sunday afternoon she plays tennis.

35. London is a long way from Delhi.

36. Unless you study hard, you will not get good marks.

37. Gopal dare not come here.

38. Have you ever been to Mumbai?

39. He wants to know as why he has been detained.

40. She is a student at the University of Jaipur.

41. As it was raining, they decided to stay indoors.

42. She arrived in Mumbai on the 15th of December.

43. We shall supply you everything you need.

44. He will phone back in ten minutes.

45. He could hardly believe his eyes.

46. It is childish to complain about rules.

47. Does your country import anything?

48. He sent for the doctor because I was ill.

49. Each of them have their own problems.

50. Will she have to pay the customs duty?

Test. 1

A part of a sentence or the entire sentence is underlined in each of the following sentences. Five alternatives are given beneath each sentence to replace the underlined part. You may choose the best alternative out of the five. These exercises are given to help you know more about the common mistakes that one often commits while writing or speaking English. The problems test the ability to recognize correct and effective expressions. Please follow the requirements of Standard Written English Grammar and choose the words and sentence construction in line with that. While choosing the answers, do not change the meaning of the original sentence. Answers are given at the end of the tests.

1. A good physician investigates not only about patients' physical health, <u>but about their mental health as well</u>.

   (a) but about their mental health too.

   (b) but about their mental health also.

   (c) but also about their mental health.

   (d) but as well as their mental health.

2. The main reason of his failing was quite evident <u>to those whom he had brought</u> into the project.

   (a) to those whom he had brought

(b) to them whom he had brought

(c) to the ones whom he had brought

(d) to those who he had brought

(e) to those who he had brought

3. She is the kind of person <u>who I think would be capable of making these kind of</u> remarks.

(a) who I think would be capable of making these kind of

(b) who I think would be capable of making these kinds of

(c) who I think would be capable of making this kind of

(d) whom I think would be capable of making these kinds of

(e) whom I think would be capable of making this kind of

4. She rose to state that <u>in her opinion, she thought, the rule should be referred back</u> to the President for amendment.

(a) in her opinion she thought the rule should be referred back

(b) she thought the rule should be referred back

(c) she thought that it must be referred back

(d)   in her opinion the rule should be referred

(e)   she thought the rule should be referred

5. Whoever <u>objects to she going to</u> the theatre should say it immediately.

(a)   objects to her going into

(b)   objects to me going to

(c)   objects to hers going to

(d)   objects to her going to

(e)   objects to she going to

6. Vinaya, the President of the Club and <u>who is also a member of the finance</u> committee, will accompany the foreign dignitary.

(a)   who is also a member of the finance committee

(b)   who is as well as a member of the finance committee

(c)   since he is a member of the finance committee

(d)   a member of the finance committee

(e)   who is a member of the finance committee as well

7. Because they cooperated <u>with one another, they divided up the work, which had been assigned.</u>

(a)   with one another, they divided up the work on the report which had been assigned.

(b) with one another, they divided the work on the report which had been assigned.

(c) they divided up the work on the report which was assigned.

(d) they divided the work on the assigned report.

(e) they divided up the work on the assigned report.

8. <u>On account of continual wind, the clouds scattered and it resulted that it did not rain</u>.

(a) As the wind continued, the clouds scattered which resulted in no rains.

(b) It did not rain because the clouds scattered on account of continued wind.

(c) On account of continual wind, the clouds got scattered and it stopped raining.

(d) On account of continued wind, the clouds scattered and resulted in not raining.

(e) As the wind continued and the clouds scattered as a consequence it stopped raining.

9. <u>Besides him, there were many people, who did not</u> approve of her odd demeanour.

(a) There were many people besides him, who did not approve of her odd demeanour.

(b) Besides him, who did not approve of her odd demeanour, there were many people.

(c) Besides many people he was also there who did not approve of her odd demeanour.

(d) Many people as well as he were there who did not approve of her odd demeanour.

(e) Besides many people, he was also there who did not approve of her odd demeanor.

10. The taxi, <u>driven by an experienced driver with an outdated engine,</u> must be sent to the workshop.

(a) driven by an experienced driver, must be sent to the workshop with an outdated engine.

(b) driven by an experienced driver, with an outdated engine, must be sent to the workshop.

(c) with an outdated engine driven by an experienced driver, must be sent to the workshop.

(d) having an outdated engine and driven by an experienced driver must be sent to the workshop.

(e) fitted with an outdated engine though driven by an experienced driver must be sent to the workshop.

11. <u>Having managed his home for many years, she understood his family better</u>.

(a) Because she managed his home for years she understood his family better.

(b) As she managed his home for many years, she understood his family better.

(c) Having managed his home for many years she could understand his family better.

(d) For many years she managed his home, so she understood his family better.

(e) Managing his home for many years she was able to understand his family better.

12. <u>Since she was living in Mumbai</u> for many years she was reluctant to move to a smaller city.

(a) As she was living in Mumbai for many years she was reluctant to move to a smaller city.

(b) Since she lived in Mumbai for many years she was reluctant to move to a smaller city.

(c) As for many years she lived in Mumbai, she was reluctant to move to a smaller city.

(d) Since she had been living in Mumbai for many years, she was reluctant to move to a smaller city.

(e) She lived in Mumbai for many years she was reluctant to move to a smaller city.

13. The Principal, <u>who was very kind spoke to the student and he</u> was very rude.

(a) who was very kind he spoke to the student who

(b) was a kind person and he spoke to the student who

(c) spoke to the student kindly and the student

(d) a kind person, spoke to the student who

(e) who was a kind person spoke to the student and he

14. Dharmpal <u>had never done it if he would have</u> known that it would hurt his parents.

(a) would have never done it if he had

(b) had done it never if he would have

(c) would have not have done it if he had

(d) would never do it if he would have

(e) had never done it if he had

15. If she is desirous to get admission in school, she should <u>submit their applications</u> before the closing date, which is June 20th.

(a) submit their application

(b) submit her application

(c) submit their applications in

(d) submit an application

(e) submit their application in

16. A good mill owner not only needs to know his workers thoroughly, <u>but requires to</u> <u>know</u> their families well.

(a) but requires to find out

(b)   but needs to find out

(c)   but also requires to know

(d)   but requires to see

(e)   but requires to meet

17. As a small boy, <u>my mother took me to Benaras to visit that holy place.</u>

   (a)   My mother took me, as a small boy, to Benaras to visit that holy place.

   (b)   My mother took me to Benaras, as a small boy, to visit that holy place.

   (c)   As a small boy, my mother took me to Benaras to visit that holy place.

   (d)   A small boy, my mother took me to Benaras to visit that holy place.

   (e)   When I was a small boy, my mother took me to Benaras to visit that holy place.

18. Too busy to pack her things herself, Sheela made a list of articles to be taken with her, ordered a working lunch, <u>went to the corner of the next building calling a taxi.</u>

   (a)   left to the corner of the next building calling a taxi.

   (b)   went to the corner of the next building and to call a taxi.

(c) went to the next building calling a taxi.

(d) went to the corner of the next building and called a taxi.

(e) went to the next building and called a taxi.

19. The shorter the speech is, it is not only welcoming, but people understand it easily too.

(a) but they understand it easily too.

(b) but people understand the speech easily.

(c) but people understand it easily.

(d) but people understand it easily as well.

(e) but people understand it also easily.

20. The collector liked the proposal and <u>it was supported by the MLA too.</u>

(a) it was supported too by the MLA.

(b) the MLA supported it too.

(c) it was supported by the MLA as well.

(d) it was supported by the MLA.

(e) it was supported also by the MLA.

1. <u>Beautifully re-varnished, John displayed the antique chair in his den.</u>

   (a) Beautiful re-varnished, John proudly displayed the antique chair in his den.

   (b) Beautifully re-varnished. John proudly displayed the antique chair in his den.

   (c) John displayed the beautifully re-varnished antique chair in his den.

   (d) An antique and beautifully re-varnished in his den John displayed the chair.

   (e) John, beautifully antique and re-varnished chair displayed in his den.

2. The most important food energy source <u>of most of the population of the world</u> <u>are grains.</u>

   (a) of most of the population of the world are grains.

   (b) for most of the population of the world are grains.

   (c) for most of the population of the world are grain.

   (d) for most of the population of the world is grain.

   (e) for the most of the population of the world are grains.

3. The probability of massive earthquakes <u>are regarded by most of the residents of the area with</u> a mixture of disbelief and caution.

   (a) are regarded by most of the residents of the area with

   (b) is regarded by most of the residents of the area with

   (c) are regarded with most residents of the area with

   (d) is regarded by most residents of the area with

   (e) are regarded by most residents of the area by

4. Everyone in the hall <u>except the small kid and me were injured</u> as the roof fell down.

   (a) except the small kid and me was injured

   (b) except the small kid and me were injured

   (c) except the small kid and me had been injured

   (d) except the small kid as well as me were injured

   (e) except me and the small kid were injured

5. <u>Neither Sheela's cousins nor her mother like</u> the guests' arrogant disposition.

   (a) Neither Sheela's cousins nor her mother liked

   (b) Sheela's cousins as well as her mother did not like

   (c) Neither Sheela's cousins nor her mother likes

    (d)   Neither Sheela's mother nor her cousins likes

    (e)   Neither Sheela's cousins and her mother does not like

6. Every candidate of the Congress Party <u>except Malik and he</u> lost the party elections.

    (a)   except Malik and his

    (b)   except Malik and him

    (c)   except Malik and himself

    (d)   except Malik and he

    (e)   except his as well as Malik

7. <u>If I were him, I would laid</u> that book on the table and keep it away from the kitchen.

    (a)   If I were he, I would lay

    (b)   If I was he, I would laid

    (c)   If I were him, I would have laid

    (d)   If I were he, I would lay

    (e)   If I was him, I would lay

8. In this commentary, <u>the writer imply that everyone who likes his idea must still</u> accept its principal theory.

    (a)   the writer imply that everyone who likes his idea must still accept its principal theory.

(b) the writer implies that everyone who likes his idea must still accept his principal theory.

(c) the writer imply that everyone whom his idea is liked must also accept its principal theory.

(d) the writer implies that everyone who like his idea must also accept his principal theory.

(f) the writer implies that everyone who likes his idea should also accept his principal theory.

9. If she <u>would have paid attention</u>, she would have not needed to be directed again.

(a) she had have paid attention,

(b) she had paid attention,

(c) she paid attention,

(d) would have paid attention,

(e) she would pay

10. He <u>is not and does not intend to play</u> again for the county cricket.

(a) is not and does not intend to play

(b) is not playing and does not intend to play

(c) is not and will not play

(d) has not and does not play

(e) has no intention nor he will play

11. The engine of the machine runs quieter when he added a heavier transmission fluid to it.

    (a) engine of the machine runs quiet

    (b) engine of the machine ran quieter

    (c) engine of the machine ran more quietly

    (d) engine of the machine will run quietly

    (e) engine of the machine ran more quietly

12. Sheetal believes that her academic achievement is better or at least as good as Meena's.

    (a) is better or at least as good as Meena's.

    (b) is as good or better than Meena.

    (c) is better or at least as good as Meena's academic records.

    (d) at least is as good as Meena's.

    (e) is better or at least as good as Meena.

13. His fortitude is as great as any other person in defending his country.

    (a) as great as any other person.

    (b) as great as other person

    (c) great like any other person

    (d) as that of any person

    (e) as great as that of any other person

14. Pradeep not only likes to work hard <u>but believes others to do hard work.</u>

   (a)   but believes that others should also work harder.

   (b)   but thinks that others to do hard work also.

   (c)   but considers that others to do hard work also.

   (d)   but also believes others to do hard work.

   (e)   but believes others to do hard work.

15. Our current Finance Minister must be honoured <u>on account their boosting up the</u> country's economy.

   (a)   on account his boosting up the country's economy.

   (b)   on account of their boosting up the country's economy.

   (c)   on account of his mates boosting up the country's economy.

   (d)   the reason being his boosting up their country's economy.

   (e)   the account of his boosting up the country's economy.

16. <u>Despite his harsh criticism of the competition</u>, the Captain reached the stage to take the trophy.

   (a)   Despite his harsh criticism of the competition,

   (b)   The competition was criticized yet,

(c)   Harshly criticizing such competitions always,

(d)   In spite of criticizing such competitions,

(e)   Criticizing very harshly all competition,

17. <u>Considering a diagnosis on the basis of insufficient or deceptive evidence</u> is neglecting years of dedicated medical training.

(a)   Considering a diagnosis on the basis of insufficient or deceptive evidence

(b)   To consider a diagnosis just to see insufficient or deceptive evidence

(c)   In view of an insufficient or deceptive evidence considering a diagnosis

(d)   Considering a diagnosis because of insufficient and deceptive evidence

(e)   In considering a diagnosis just because of insufficient or deceptive evidence

18. While many members of the Party may feel powerless to influence the Secretary about the policy matters, <u>it is truly effective to write to him with an opinion.</u>

(a)   it is truly effective to write to him with an opinion.

(b)   writing to the Secretary with an opinion is actually effective.

(c)   to write to the secretary with an opinion is effective.

(d)   writing of an opinion to the Secretary may be effective.

19. Dr Radhakrishnan was a professor of Philosophy at the University of Madras, <u>at the same time also one of India's greatest President.</u>

(a)   at the same time also one of India's greatest President.

(b)   and at the same time was also one of India's greatest Presidents.

(c)   at the same time as he was India's great President.

(d)   at the same time was also one of India's greatest Presidents.

(e)   being one of India's greatest president at the same time.

20. Having been asked by the magistrate to pay the fine, Nitin <u>was still not required by it to pay</u>.

(a)   Nitin was still not required by it to pay.

(b)   Nitin was further not required by it to pay the fine.

(c)   Nitin was never required to pay the fine.

(d)   Nitin was still not required to pay.

(e)   Nitin was hardly required by it to pay.

Miscellaneous Sentences

At the top of each sentence, the area of the error is indicated.

<u>The area of error:</u> *Subject and verb must always agree.*

1. Her cat, <u>along with her dog and the goldfish, don't permit</u> her to take long trips.

   (a) along with her dog and the goldfish , don't permit

   (b) as well as her dog and goldfish, doesn't permit

   (c) together with her dog and goldfish, are not permitting

   (d) accompanied by her dog and goldfish, don't permit

   (e) in addition to her dog and goldfish, don't permit

Pronoun must agree with the words they refer to

2. The teacher said <u>that everyone will bring home-made foodstuff from their home.</u>

   (a) that everyone will bring home-made foodstuff from their home.

   (b) that everyone must bring home-made foodstuff from his home.

   (c) that everyone must bring homemade foodstuff from one's home.

(d)   that everyone must bring homemade foodstuff from her home

(e)   that all of us must bring homemade foodstuff from their home.

Pronouns must be in the correct case

3. The judges were requested <u>to award the scholarships to whomever got the highest</u> marks.

(a)   to award the scholarships to whomever got the highest marks.

(b)   to award the scholarships to whomever gets the highest marks.

(c)   to award the scholarships to whoever got the highest marks.

(d)   to award the scholarships to whom got the highest marks.

(e)   to award the scholarships to whose marks were high.

Tenses (verb) must reflect the sequence of events.

4. When he opened the hood of his van and saw smoke coming from the engine, he <u>realized that he forgot to add engine oil</u>.

(a)   realized that he forgot to add engine oil.

(b)   realized that he forgets to add engine oil.

(c)   realized that he forgot to add some engine oil.

(d)   realized that he had forgotten to add engine oil.

(e)   had realized that he forgot to add engine oil.

A pronoun modifying a gerund must be in the possessive case

5. <u>She disapproves of you insisting that the books were misplaced on purpose.</u>

(a)   She disapproves of you that the books were misplaced on purpose.

(b)   She disapproves of you insisting that the books were purposely misplaced.

(c)   She disapproves of your insisting that the books were misplaced on purpose.

(d)   She does not approve of you insisting that the books were misplaced purposefully.

(e)   She disapprove of your insisting that the books were misplaced on purpose.

Comparisons must be logical

6. <u>A teacher's physical impact including gestures, body and facial impressions is</u> as important as listening to his lectures.

(a)   A teacher's physical impact including gestures, body and facial impressions is

◆ 137 ◆

(b) A teacher's physical impact gestures, facial impressions and body carriage are

(c) A teacher's physical, body and facial impressions are

(d) To examine a teacher's physical impact and body and facial impressions are

(e) Examining a teacher's physical, body and facial impressions are

Modifiers must stay close to home

7. <u>By leading trump, the proposal was defeated flatly by the defenders.</u>

(a) By leading trump, the proposal was defeated flatly by the defenders.

(b) By leading trump, the defenders defeated the proposal flatly.

(c) The defenders flatly defeated the proposal by leading trump.

(d) The proposal, by leading trump, was defeated flatly by the defenders.

(e) Flatly, the proposal was defeated by the defenders by leading trump.

Sentence fragments don't cut it (When a sentence does not contain a subject or verb *it is not a complete sentence no matter how long a phrase it contains.*)

8. The lovesick girl was very doleful as <u>the boy who she loved and who had left her for another girl.</u>

   (a) the boy who she loved and who had left her for another girl.

   (b) the boy whom she loved and whom had left her for another girl.

   (c) the boy whom she loved and who had left her for another girl.

   (d) the boy whom she loved had left her for another girl.

   (e) the boy who she loved had left her for another girl.

Run on sentences don't make it. (The following sentence is an example of a run-on *sentence. It is a sentence that contains two independent clauses which are not joined properly.)*

9. At the outset, Sadhana was the group's leader, <u>later on it occurred to the group that</u> Seema was more capable and more agile.

   (a) later on it occurred to the group that

   (b) that was not the better thing to reckon with

   (c) but the group came to realize that

   (d) the group concluded, however, that

   (e) then the group decided that

We don't start a sentence with because.

10. <u>Because she does not agree with you</u> it does not indicate that she does not like you.

    (a) Because she does not agrees with you

    (b) If she does not agrees with you

    (c) Because you and she does not agree with

    (d) When she does not agree with you

    (e) That she does not agree with you

Choose the right word. (Don't get trapped by making a needless change unless you *have a good reason for it.* Faulty diction is often a big problem.)

11. <u>The unlawful students were expedited from one place to the other</u> for reformation.

    (a) The unlawful students were expedited from one place to another

    (b) From one place to another the unlawful students were expedited

    (c) The unlawful students were expedited to another place

    (d) The unlawful students were extradited from one place to another

    (e) The unlawful students from one to another place were expedited

Wordy answer choices are no solutions. Please don't choose answers just because they sound 'important.'

12. If one starts drinking at an early age, <u>it is possible that he will go on drinking in</u> <u>future.</u>

    (a) it is possible that he will go on drinking in future.

    (b) it is possible that he will go on drinking forever.

    (c) he will probably go on drinking more and more.

    (d) it is hard to stop him from drinking more in future.

    (e) he is likely to continue drinking.

Misplaced Modifiers. Misplaced modifiers come in several forms. A few examples are given below.

(i) Remember that when a sentence begins with a *participial phrase*, it is supposed to modify the noun or pronoun immediately it follows.

13. <u>Coming out of the office</u> <u>Satish's valuables was robbed</u>.

    (a) Coming out of the office, Satish's valuables was robbed.

    (b) Coming out of the office, Satish was robbed of his valuables.

    (c) In coming out of the office, Satish's valuables were robbed.

    (d) While Satish left the office someone had robbed him of his valuables.

    (e)   Satish was coming out of the office, someone robbed his valuables.

14. <u>On leaving the office Satish's valuables were robbed.</u>

(ii) When a *participial phrase* is preceded by a preposition, it must modify the noun or pronoun.

    (a)   On leaving the office Satish's valuables were robbed.

    (b)   While Satish left the office he was robbed of his valuables.

    (c)   When Satish came out of the office someone robbed his valuables.

    (d)   As Satish left the office, his valuables were robbed.

    (e)   On leaving the office, Satish was robbed of his valuables.

15. <u>Before designing a building, the owner of the building must be considered.</u>

(iii) A close relative of a misplaced modifier is a *dangling modifier*. It can be identified in an easy way.

    (a)   Before designing a building the owner of the building must be considered.

    (b)   The owner of the building must be considered before designing the building.

    (c)   Before designing a building, the architect must consider its owner.

(d)   The owner needs to be consulted before any building is designed.

(e)   When a building is designed, it is necessary that its owner must be considered.

Answers

Test. 1

1. (e) *but also*

2. (a) *No error*

3. (b) is *correct, as an adjective* should agree in number with the noun *it modifies. 'who' is the right choice*

4. (e) words *in her opinion* & *back* are not required

5. (d) the correct use the pronoun is *her* and not *she*

6. (d) words like *'who is also,'* are superfluous.

7. (d) *It's the precise and* to the point expression.

8. (b) *it seems to be the most befitting expression*

9. (a) *It's the most appropriate and to the point expression.*

10. (b) *two commas put after driver and engine provide better sense.*

11. (b) *It provides the best meaning and sense. Normally, we don't start a sentence with* because.

12. (d) *Past perfect tense is* correct in this case.

13. (d) *It's a more precise and* to the point expression.

14. (a) *It makes the sentence past conditional,* which is the correct usage in this case.

15. (d) *As she is singular, it will* not take 'their' application.

16. (c) *'not only' is followed by 'but also'.*

17. (e) *It corrects the modifier* as a small boy, referring to *my mother incorrectly.*

18. (d) *verb in the last clause/sentence* should have the same tense.

19. (e) *not only* goes with *but also.*

20. (b) *Where it is possible, use active voice only.*

Test. 2

1. (c) It provides the best and the most accurate sense.

2. (d) It is not 'of' but *for* is correct. *Is,* is the only correct form as it agrees with the number with its subject. Again, it is grain and not grains which is acceptable.

3. (d) *is* the only nearest correct form as it is not 'are' but 'is' that agrees with the subject 'possibility.'

4. (a) Everyone is always considered to be a singular indefinite pronoun. Therefore, it will have 'was' and not were.

5. (c) is correct as there is a rule that when two distinct words or phrases are joined by the correlative either...or, neither...nor, or not only but also, the number (singular or plural) of the word or phrase nearer to the verb decides the number of the verb. The verb liked cannot be used as it changes the tense and the meaning of the sentence.

6. (b) is correct as *except* is a proposition so it should take an object *him* and not a subject he.

7. (d) is correct because pronoun on both sides of the verb should be a subject. So the use of 'he' is correct.

8. (b) is correct. The word writer being singular, it will take a singular verb 'implies.' Again, 'its' is a wrong choice as it refers to the author, so it should take 'his' and not 'its.'

9. (b) is correct because the event of paying attention actually would have occurred earlier than her being directed for it again. Therefore, the event that was to take place earlier will have the verb *had* and the other one will *have would* have.

10. (b) is the correct answer. The sentence contains an example of an ellipsis (omission of a word or words from a sentence) in some form. It is the word 'playing' after is that is missing.

11. (c) is correct. The error in the sentence is the use of the verb quieter (the adjective form of quiet). The word quieter modifies the verb runs therefore, it should take the correct form of the adverb 'more quietly', rather than quieter.

12. (c) is the correct alternative. The word 'than' is essential to be used as two items are being compared.

13. (e) is the correct answer because it clearly shows comparison between his fortitude and that of the any other person's fortitude.

14. (d) is correct as 'not only' takes 'but also' in the next clause.

15. (a) is the only correct form as it takes the correct pronoun 'his' instead of 'their' which is misplaced.

16. (a) is the only correct choice as it makes the sense well.

17. (a) is the most suitable choice as it is a clear expression in itself.

   Therefore, there is no error in the sentence.

18. (b) Is the correct answer. The original sentence is not logical. It implies that one should write to the Secretary who has an opinion. The answer 'b' eliminates this ambiguity.

19. (d) is the only correct option. The original sentence runs two distinct ideas together. 'B' separates the two ideas

and puts it in such a way that both have equal weight.

20. (d) is the correct choice as it does not take 'by it' which is not required in the sentence.

Test. 3

Miscellaneous Exercises

1. (b) is the only correct answer as the verb 'don't' doesn't match with the subject 'her cat', which is in singular.

2. (c) is the correct answer as it refers to each one's home (one's home). Everyone being singular in number it must take a singular pronoun which it refers to. Although (b) also looks to be correct, but (c) is more accurate than (b) as everyone has a neutral gender, so 'one's home' is more correct.

3. (c) is the correct answer as the correct pronoun to be used is *whoever* and not whomever.

4. (d) is the correct answer as adding the engine oil should have preceded than to realizing that he forgot to add engine oil. The event that took place first will have 'had' and the second clause will simply be in the past tense.

5. (c) is the only correct answer as it has the pronoun *your*, (modifying the gerund insisting) in possessive case.

6. (e) seems to be the only nearest correct answer. The sentence as it is there, makes a comparison between

impact and listening, which is grammatically incorrect. In fact 'examining' is closer to listening therefore (e) is the only correct answer under the circumstances.

7. (c) is the only correct choice as it corrects the error of the misplaced modifier.

8. (d) is the only correct alternative as it makes a complete sense. The underlined portion of this sentence is a fragment because it contains a subject (boy) but no verb to act as a predicate for the subject. Besides 'whom' is the correct possessive pronoun than 'who' which is just an error to do use.

9. (c) is the only correct alternative. The portion of the sentence before the comma is an independent clause which can work as a complete sentence. So is the case with the part after the comma. A comma by itself is not sufficient to separate two independent clauses. It therefore requires a coordinating conjunction such *as and, but, yet, or, nor*, etc. The choice (c) provides such a conjunction.

10. (e) is the only correct choice as none of the other choices can act as the subject of the sentence. In fact, the omission of *The fact* from the choice 'e' is another example of an ellipsis.

11. (d)In this sentence, the word expedited has been incorrectly used as it means 'speed up' or 'hastened.' The proper word to choose in the context is extradited,

which means to surrender from one place to another. Thus, choice 'd' is correct.

12. (e) is correct. It is an example of unnecessary wordy original sentence. While you shorten a wordy sentence, you must remember that you don't change the meaning of the sentence. In view of that, the choice (e) is the only correct choice. It not only reduces the size of the sentence, but also doesn't change its meaning.

13. (b) is the correct choice in view of the rule stated just after the sentence.

14. (e) Under the circumstances and keeping in view the rule it is the only correct option.

15. (c) is the correct choice under the rule. The dangling modifier does not, in fact, modify any word. So to fix this sentence you need to insert whoever (the architect) designed the building.

OO

Test Paper

1. The number of people jogging in city parks, in playgrounds, and even in the streets, <u>is at least five times what they were</u> only five years ago.

   (a) is at least five times what they were

   (b) are at least five times what they had been

   (c) is at least five times what it was

   (d) are at least five times what it was

   (e) is at least five times than what the numbers were

2. For some children, <u>accepting parental discipline that they consider unfair, constitute</u> a necessary accommodation.

   (a) accepting parental discipline that they consider unfair, constitute

   (b) acceding to parental discipline which they consider unfair, constitute

   (c) accepting parental discipline that one considers unfair, constitute

   (d) to accept parental discipline what they consider unfair, constitute

   (e) accepting parental discipline which they consider unfair, constitutes

3. To protest their being underpaid in comparison to other city agencies, a strike was called by the paramedical workers.

   (a) To protest their being underpaid in comparison to other city agencies, a strike was called by the paramedical workers.

   (b) To protest them being underpaid in comparison with other city agencies, the paramedical workers called a strike.

   (c) To protest their being comparatively underpaid with other city agencies, a strike was called by the paramedical workers.

   (d) To protest their being underpaid in comparison with workers of other city agencies, the paramedical workers called a strike.

   (e) The paramedical workers called a strike to protest them being underpaid in comparison with other city workers.

4. The parties have an agreement in principle, <u>and because there is no</u> signed contract does not mean that they cannot commence doing business immediately.

   (a) and because there is no

   (b) and there being no

   (c) so an absent

(d) so the lack of a

(e) therefore no

5. The committee rejected the proposal for several reasons, <u>the chief among which were the cost of borrowing the money.</u>

   (a) the chief among which were the cost of borrowing the money

   (b) the chief among which was the cost of borrowing the money

   (c) the chief of which was the cost of borrowing the money

   (d) the chief were the cost of borrowing the money

   (e) with the cost of borrowing money being the one of them

6. To be fair, it was Finance Minister P. Chidambaram who suggested the changeover on the grounds that "Vibrancy of the equity market <u>must be extended to the debt market on moving to a screen-based trading platform".</u>

   (a) must be extended to the debt market on moving to a screen-based trading platform".

   (b) ought to be extended to the debt market by moving to a screen-based trading platform".

   (c) must extend to the debt market on moving to a screen-based trading platform".

(d) must have been extended to the debt market on moving to a screen-based trading platform".

7. The employment contracts of most high-level managers contain so-called Golden Parachute <u>clauses, under which the executive is guaranteed</u> substantial compensation if their firms ever fall victim to a hostile takeover.

   (a) clauses, under which the executive is guaranteed

   (b) clauses that guarantee these executives

   (c) clauses, guaranteeing that these executives

   (d) clause, under which the executive is guaranteed of

   (e) clause that guarantee the executive of

8. Mahabharat has often been described as a great story told greatly.

   (a) Mahabharat has often been described as a great story told greatly.

   (b) Mahabharat has been described as a great story often told greatly.

   (c) Often told greatly, Mahabharat has been described as a great story.

   (d) Told greatly, Mahabharat is often described as a great story.

   (e) A great story, Mahabharat is often described as greatly told.

9. The portfolio, which was apparently <u>left inadvertent at home, contained three completed watercolours,</u> including several uncompleted sketches.

(a) left inadvertent at home, contained three completed watercolours, including several uncompleted sketches.

(b) left inadvertently at home, contained three completed watercolours, including several uncompleted sketches.

(c) inadvertently left at home containing three completed watercolours, including several uncompleted sketches.

(d) left inadvertently at home with three completed watercolours and several uncompleted sketches.

(e) inadvertently left at home, contained three completed watercolours and several uncompleted sketches.

10. Although the stock market offer the possibility of great personal gain, you must understand that to invest in stocks <u>is accepting the risk of financial ruin as well.</u>

(a) is accepting the risk of financial ruin as well.

(b) is to accept the risk of financial ruin as well.

(c) is to accept the risk as well as financial ruin.

(d) are accepting the risk of financial ruin as well.

(e) Are to expect the risk of financial ruin as well.

11. Political games are played over river waters in the north too. Only last week, the president <u>seeked the Supreme Court's opinion on whether law makers in Punjab are</u> right in rejecting an agreement to share Sutlej waters with Haryana.

   (a) seeked the Supreme Court's opinion on whether law makers in Punjab are

   (b) seeked the Supreme Court's opinion on whether law makers in Punjab have the

   (c) sought the Supreme Court's opinion on whether law makers in Punjab were

   (d) sought the Supreme Court's opinion on whether law makers in Punjab are

12. Concrete is an artificial material made from a mixture of port land cement, water, fine and coarse aggregates, <u>having a small</u> amount of air.

   (a) having a small

   (b) having added a small

   (c) adding a small

   (d) and a little

   (e) and a small

13. Although today it is easy to make perfumes with synthetic ingredients, <u>they used to make the classic fragrances from flowers only</u> and other natural essences.

   (a)   they used to make the classic fragrances from flowers only

   (b)   the classic fragrances used to be made only from flowers

   (c)   the classic fragrances used to be made by them only from flowers

   (d)   the classic fragrances ought to be made from flowers only

   (e)   only flowers were used for making the classic fragrances

14. Americans give pride of place to the value of individual liberty, and we find <u>especially unintelligible the infliction of suffering</u> on the innocent.

   (a)   especially unintelligible the infliction of suffering

   (b)   especial unintelligible the fiction of suffering

   (c)   especially unintelligible suffrage that is inflicted

   (d)   especially unintelligible the suffering that is inflicted

   (e)   specially illegible infliction of suffering

15. The revelation that Shakespeare wrote certain of his plays expressly for Queen Elizabeth I lends credence to

the theory that the dark lady of the sonnets was <u>not</u> <u>Shakespeare's mistress nor any other woman the</u> <u>playwright had romanced</u> but, infact, the Queen herself.

(a) not Shakespeare's mistress nor any other woman the playwright had romanced

(b) neither Shakespeare's mistress or any other woman the playwright had romanced

(c) neither Shakespeare's mistress nor any other woman the playwright had romanced

(d) not Shakespeare's mistress or any other woman the playwright had romanced

(e) not Shakespeare's mistress neither any other woman he had romanced

16. Many travellers state unequivocally <u>that the streets in</u> <u>Delhi are more beautiful than any other city.</u>

(a) that the streets in Delhi are more beautiful than any other city.

(b) that the streets in Delhi are more beautiful than those in any other city.

(c) that Delhi streets are more beautiful than in any other city.

(d) that unlike any other city, Delhi streets are more beautiful.

(e) that the streets of Delhi are more beautiful than the streets in any other city.

17. Assigning additional work to an already overburdened worker, <u>one made often by inept managers, it increases the risk</u> that the worker will become totally alienated and cease being productive altogether.

(a) one made often by inept managers, it increases the risk

(b) one often made by inept managers, increases the risk

(c) a mistake often made by inept managers, the risk rises

(d) a mistake often made by inept managers, increases the risk

(e) which is often done by inept managers, the risk is increased that

18. Although the reaction to initial marketing surveys was not favourable, the growing acceptance by consumers <u>seem to indicate the product will ultimately be very popular.</u>

(a) seem to indicate the product will ultimately be very popular

(b) seem to indicate the ultimate popularity of the product

(c) seems to indicate that the product will ultimately be very popular

(d) are indicating that the product will ultimately be very popular

(e) seems to be an indication as to the ultimately popularity of the product

19. The number of adults in the United States who are illiterate is <u>rising, but it is probably only temporary.</u>

(a) rising, but it is probably only temporary

(b) rising, but it is only temporary

(c) rising, but it is temporary only

(d) rising, but the increase is probably only a temporary one

(e) rising, although the increase may only be temporarily

20. The prospects of rich countries <u>to discover the virtue of altruism seems</u> quite slim at the moment.

(a) to discover the virtue of altruism seems

(b) discovering the virtue of altruism seem

(c) having discovered the virtue of altruism seems

(d) on discovering the virtue of altruism seem

21. Fidel Castro found it simple to seize power, but <u>maintaining it difficult.</u>

(a) maintaining it difficult

(b) its maintenance difficult

(c) difficult to maintain it

(d) difficulty was experienced in maintaining it

(e) difficulty in as much as maintaining it was concerned

22. Results of the recent study make it mandatory that the Medical Superintendent <u>rejects</u> implementation of the experimental procedure.

(a) rejects

(b) should reject

(c) reject

(d) must reject

(e) will reject

23. The *munshi* told me that the lawyer's office closes at 5:00 P.M.

(a) The *munshi* told me that the lawyer's office closes at 5:00 P.M.

(b) The *munshi* told me that the lawyer's office had closed at 5:00 P.M.

(c) The *munshi* had told me that the lawyer's office had closed at 5:00 P.M.

(d) The *munshi* told me that lawyer's office would have to close at 5:00 P.M.

24. Smart investors saw early on that the compact disk, on which music is recorded in a digital code to be read by a laser, would soon become the most common form of recorded <u>music, eventually replacing</u> records and tapes altogether.

   (a) music, eventually replacing

   (b) music, and eventually replacing

   (c) music that eventually replaces

   (d) music by eventually replacing

   (e) music to eventually replace

25. Tibetan rugs are so expensive because <u>the weaver still pursues his art as they have</u> for centuries, by hand-dyeing all their wool and then knotting each thread individually to achieve a unique pattern for every piece.

   (a) the weaver still pursues his art as they have

   (b) the weaver still pursues his art as he has

   (c) weavers still pursue their art as they have

   (d) weavers still pursue their art as was done

   (e) the weaver still pursues his art as has been done

26. The exclusive Taj restaurant has been popular with business customers <u>because of its excellent service,</u>

responsive management, and because its parking facilities are extensive.

(a) because of its excellent service, responsive management, and because its parking facilities are extensive.

(b) Because of its excellent service, responsive management, and because their parking facilities are extensive.

(c) Because of its service, which is excellent, management, which is responsive, and because of parking facilities which are extensive.

(d) Because of its excellent service, responsive management and extensive parking facilities.

(e) Because of its excellent service, responsive management and its extensive parking facilities.

27. Politics apart, it is time EU goes back to common sense economic policies if it was to remain a force to reckon with.

(a) goes back to common sense economic policies if it was

(b) goes back to common sense economic policies if it is

(c) went back to common sense economic policies if it is

(d)   went back to common sense economic policies if it was

28. Since they shared so much when they were growing up, Neena and Juhi have cultivated a very special friendship and even now confide their most intimate thoughts only <u>to one another.</u>

(a)   to one another

(b)   one with the other

(c)   one with another

(d)   each to the other

(e)   to each other

29. A survey of business schools concludes that <u>female students are more concerned about job discrimination than male students.</u>

(a)   female students are more concerned about job discrimination than male students

(b)   female students are more concerned about job discrimination than male students are

(c)   female students, as opposed to male students, are more concerned about job discrimination

(d)   female students are more concerned about job discrimination than male students are concerned

(e) female students are more concerned about job discrimination than their male counterparts.

30. <u>To lack self-discipline is to lack</u> any true commitment to the goals one has set.

   (a) To lack self-discipline is to lack

   (b) To be lacking in self-discipline is to lack

   (c) To lack self-discipline must be to lack

   (d) Lacking self-discipline is to be lacking

   (e) Lacking self-discipline is the lack of

31. Married woman raising young children do not respond to social stresses <u>as poorly as unmarried women do.</u>

   (a) as poorly as unmarried women do

   (b) as much as unmarried women do

   (c) as poorly as unmarried women

   (d) as much as unmarried women have

   (e) as well as unmarried women

32. They pay attention to small details, eliminate problems at the source and <u>trimming anything resembling excess, whether it is</u> work, code or material.

   (a) trimming anything resembling excess, whether it is

   (b) trim anything resembling excess, whether it is

(c) trim anything resembling excess, whether it was

(d) trim anything resembling excess, whether it be

33. <u>Inspite of forbidden by Church law to marry, it was not unusual for a priest during the Middle Ages to sire a family</u>.

(a) Inspite of forbidden by Church law to marry, it was not unusual for a priest during the Middle Ages to sire a family.

(b) Forbidden by Church law to marry, it was quite normal for a priest during the Middle Ages to sire a family.

(c) Though they were forbidden by Church law to marry, it was usual for him during the Middle Ages to sire a family.

(d) Although they were forbidden by Church law to marry, it was not unusual for priests during the Middle Ages to sire families.

OO

Answers

1. (c); 2. (e); 3. (d); 4. (d); 5. (c); 6. (b); 7. (b); 8. (a);
9. (e); 10. (b); 11. (c); 12. (e); 13. (b); 14. (a); 15. (c);
16. (b); 17. (d); 18. (c); 19. (d); 20. (b); 21. (c); 22. (c);
23. (a); 24. (a); 25. (c); 26. (e); 27. (c); 28. (e); 29. (b);
30. (a); 31. (a); 32. (d); 33. (d).

OO

English is a unique language which has innumerable great poets and authors from the past as well as the present, who have contributed profusely to its rich heritage. Nonetheless, we cannot ignore the complexities of the English language which sometimes perplex a reader or even a scholar of this language.

Improve Your Word Power by Clifford Sawhney simplifies all these complexities of the language by providing answers to the many nagging grammatical queries, syntax, style, choice of words, spellings, etc. This book serves as a complete guide and elaborately explains the different usages of nouns, adjectives, adverbs, phrases, proverbs and so on. Hence, it will undoubtedly serve as a bible for both the lovers and wizards of English language.

Pages: 232 • Price: Rs. 80/- • Postage: Rs. 15/-

The book aims to display uncommon expressions that look common but are uncommon in usage and meaning. The uncommon expressions are interwoven within he conversations fitted into suitable situations. Dialogues containing common and uncommon expressions, phrases and idioms are developed in a most fascinating style displaying a rich vocabulary and appropriate language that provides a modern touch. In this respect, the reader will have a face chance to experience varied and trying situations during different sets of conversations.

The book not only provides new vistas of vision as regards learning how to converse with the people, but also extends before the reader new sets of situations knitted in dialogues enabling one to enrich his/her linguistic capabilities.

Pages: 136 • Price: Rs. 50/- • Postage: Rs. 15/-